Inspirational Female Sports Stories for Kids

Jessica Blakely

© Copyright 2024 - All rights reserved.

The content contained within this book may not be reproduced, duplicated or transmitted without direct written permission from the author or the publisher.

Under no circumstances will any blame or legal responsibility be held against the publisher, or author, for any damages, reparation, or monetary loss due to the information contained within this book, either directly or indirectly.

Legal Notice:

This book is copyright protected. It is only for personal use. You cannot amend, distribute, sell, use, quote or paraphrase any part, or the content within this book, without the consent of the author or publisher.

Disclaimer Notice:

Please note the information contained within this book is for educational and entertainment purposes only. All effort has been executed to present accurate, up to date, reliable, complete information. No warranties of any kind are declared or implied. Readers acknowledge that the author is not engaged in the rendering of legal, financial, medical or professional advice. The content within this book has been derived from various sources. Please consult a licensed professional before attempting any techniques outlined in this book.

By reading this document, the reader agrees that under no circumstances is the author responsible for any losses, direct or indirect, that are incurred as a result of the use of the information contained within this document, including, but not limited to, errors, omissions, or inaccuracies.

Contents

Introduction	1
Serena Williams	5
Leah Williamson	13
Simone Biles	21
Chloe Kim	29
Ibtihaj Muhammad	37
Maya Moore	45
Jackie Joyner-Kersee	53
Megan Rapinoe	63
Tatyana McFadden	71
Bethany Hamilton	81
Wilma Rudolph	89
Hilary Knight	97
Conclusion	105
Dear Wonderful Parents	107
References	109

Introduction

"If at first you don't succeed, try and try again!"

Have you heard this quote before? It is probably one of the most famous motivational quotes of all time. It has been used by poets, teachers, kings, speakers, and many others for hundreds of years! So, it must be important, right?

One of the most famous times this quote was used is in the legend of the Scottish king, Robert the Bruce. After the King of England's army defeated him, Robert ran away and hid in a cave. Frightened and upset that he had lost, Robert watched a spider spinning its web in a dark corner of his cave.

The spider tried to connect its web from one side of the cave wall to the other, but it fell down. Robert watched it climb back up and try again – but again, it fell.

Both times, the spider returned to the cave wall and tried again. It never gave up, even though it might have been easier to make a smaller web or try again somewhere else. Each time the spider failed to complete its web, it climbed back up and tried again.

On its third try, the spider was successful and managed to build a beautiful web. It could finally rest peacefully in the middle of its new home. Robert could not believe what he had seen. The spider had been so determined, and instead of giving up, it kept trying repeatedly until the web worked. It was a lot like his own trials in battle.

Inspired by the spider's determination, Robert left the cave. He returned to his army, and took back his land. It took him a long time, but like the spider, Robert kept trying again and again until he succeeded. He refused to give up, and he went on to beat his enemy.

We don't know where the idea of "If at first you don't succeed, try and try again!" came from, but it doesn't matter. The importance of it is the same: Don't give up. If you fail, get up and try again. This saying is useful for anyone who faces difficulties.

We all have moments when it feels like we cannot go further. We all have moments when it feels like we have failed too many times to ever succeed, but this is simply not true!

Take athletes, for example. People who play sports know better than anyone else how important it is to keep going even when things get tough. They are always practicing because they know that sometimes, making mistakes helps them to get better.

If you have ever played a sport, then you know that it doesn't feel great when your team loses after you've practiced every day for weeks. But does that stop your team from practicing again? No! You keep practicing to make sure you get better after that loss. And this is exactly what Robert the Bruce found out: sometimes, we have to lose a couple of times before we are able to win.

We can actually learn a lot from sports, even if we aren't players ourselves. And we can especially learn a lot from female athletes. They face some of the hardest challenges in life because they are women.

You see, some people believe that women are weaker than men, no matter how many times history has proven this idea wrong. That means it can be tough to chase your dreams if you're a girl, because lots of people don't believe in you. But as you will see throughout this book, women who work hard can do whatever they set their minds to!

INTRODUCTION

Did you know that there were 1,066 athletes in the 1900 Olympic Games? Did you know that only 12 of them were women? Only 12 out of over a thousand people! And before the year 1900, it was rare to ever see a woman playing any kind of sport anywhere.

Women who play sports today have overcome many challenges so that they can compete too. Sportswomen throughout history have fought against unfair laws and wrong opinions with courage and determination. They are the ultimate example of never giving up, even when it feels like you've failed.

In this book, you will read many inspiring stories about female athletes who overcame challenges like this to achieve their dreams and goals. But you know what the best thing about these stories is?

They teach us that winning isn't the most important thing. The most important thing is the journey that shapes who you are and makes you the best person you can be. The lessons we learn from failing are sometimes more important than the fun of winning.

You'll see over and over again in these stories how each woman had many challenges placed in their path, making it hard for them to succeed. But over and over again, you'll see how these women refused to let those things stop them from achieving their dreams.

If you're struggling to understand how you could possibly be like one of these great female athletes, remember that they were once just like you. They were once a little girl with a big dream and used these same lessons to get to where they are today.

Think about it: if you try out for a team but you don't get the spot, then you know to practice harder for the next try-outs. If you fail a test, then you know to study harder for the next one. One failure is only a setback, not the end. Because when you really want something, you are worthy of having it. You just have to work hard to get it.

Those are the things that these women teach us.

From tennis stars to soccer heroines, you will read many stories of different situations and the ways these women found strength even when it was hard. They all started out wanting to succeed. They all had different obstacles in their ways, and it was hard to get to the top. Along the way, they each learned that winning is far less important than determination, fair play, teamwork, and respect.

Many of these 12 athletes faced problems to do with their skin color, their family backgrounds, or their disabilities, but they each found a way to embrace who they are. They each made the choice to keep going, no matter what life threw at them. In the end, this is exactly what makes them so inspirational.

I hope that as you read these strong women's stories, you find moments of their lives that are similar to yours. While the world now knows them as super-powerful athletes, they had to learn each lesson one at a time, one failure at a time. Like you, they grew up making mistakes, failing, and feeling like they'd never make it to their goals. But they kept going, and if that worked for them, then you can make it too.

You'll soon see that the lessons these women learned can apply to anything you want to do. Whether you want to get better grades, feel more confident, make public speeches, win sports competitions, or just conquer your fears, you can learn a lot from these women and their hard work. Maybe you can use their examples to overcome problems and accomplish your dreams, just as they did. Who knows? Maybe you'll be the next one to inspire others!

Remember, through struggle, we become stronger! Serena Williams is a famous tennis player who once said, "I don't like to lose – at anything – yet I've grown most not from victories, but setbacks." She knew that it was the failures that made her stronger, and that's true for you too!

Serena Williams

Once upon a time, in the heartland of America, lived a young girl with big dreams of becoming a professional tennis player. Her name was Serena.

Serena was born on September 26, 1981, in Compton, California, to Richard and Oracene Williams. She had a sister called Venus, who was one year older than her. It was not easy growing up in Compton, because there was a lot of crime. It was not known for superstar athletes.

But luckily for Serena, her father saw potential in her and her older sister, Venus. When Serena was only three years old, her father started teaching her how to play tennis. That's right! Serena was very little when she first held a tennis racket. It was probably as big as she was!

From that point on, Serena and Venus practiced every day with their father. He didn't have much experience with tennis, but he was convinced that his daughters could be very good at it. He taught himself how to play tennis by reading books and watching videos, and he helped his daughters learn too.

However, Compton was not the greatest place to teach Serena. The only tennis courts the family could practice on were in a bad state. They were filled with broken glass, and there was a lot of crime. And African American families like Serena's have often been unwelcome in sports, simply due to the color of their skin.

But Serena was determined to be the best. Even though tennis was thought to be a "White-person sport," Serena and her father ignored any unkind comments and kept practicing. She refused to listen to those who wanted to make her feel bad just because she was a Black girl instead of White. So, she practiced with old rackets on cracked courts until she could play better than anyone who dared challenge her!

Finally, the family moved from Compton to Florida so that she and Venus could go to Rick Macci's Tennis Academy and become even better tennis players. And even though Serena and her sister practiced hard at the academy, their father also kept coaching them at home. He really wanted them to be the best! Eventually, Serena's father became their only teacher again so he could make sure they were getting all the training they needed.

Training to become a tennis player taught Serena how to be focused. And it paid off! By the age of ten, Serena was named the top player in her age group by the United States Tennis Association. That kind of achievement takes lots of hard work and determination!

When she felt unwell or defeated in any way, she would just get up and try again. Later in life, she said, "With a defeat, when you lose, you get up, you make it better, you try again. That's what I do in life, when I get down, when I get sick, I don't want to just stop. I keep going, and I try to do more. Everyone says never give up, but you really have to take that to heart and really do never definitely give up. Keep trying."

Serena tried and tried again as she began her professional career when she was just 14. She did not win every tennis match she played, but she continued to work hard and get better. Serena's older sister was also starting to play tennis professionally.

Many people expected Venus to win a big tennis competition first, but nope! It was Serena! When she was just 18 years old, Serena won the US Open Championships in Queens, New York. Instead of being jealous of Serena's impressive win, Venus just cheered her sister on. A few years later, they even won the doubles category of the tournament together!

They often played as a team, which is called playing doubles in tennis. They were unstoppable! They won gold medals for their teamwork in doubles at the 2000 Sydney Olympics, but they still had their own goals too. Serena's career as a solo player would soon become one of the most impressive in the history of tennis.

At the 2002 Wimbledon Championships, another huge international championship, Serena showed the world just what she could do. Serena and Venus both played singles, which meant they had to play against each other. Can you imagine having to play against your older sister in a professional tournament? I can't!

Well, she not only defeated her own sister, but won the whole competition! This made Serena the number 1 female tennis player in the whole world! That's a huge deal. On top of that, she was only the third African American to earn that title. What an achievement for women and African American players everywhere!

That day, Serena Williams became an example to other female players, showing that a person's determination and hard work are the things that make them great. Nothing other than that matters.

Serena showed the world that Black tennis players can play just as well as — or perhaps better than — their White competitors. Serena showed that she was *proud* to be a Black woman, which was uncommon.

During a later tennis match, Serena and Venus chose to wear their hair in beaded braids, a hairstyle specific to the African American community, to show their pride in who they are. Before this moment, Black players had been expected to wear their hair like their White opponents. Serena decided that was nonsense and chose to wear her hair as she wanted.

And they did not stop at just that. Serena was determined to challenge the expectations of both female and Black athletes. She wanted to show everyone that tennis should not be about skin color or gender but about sportsmanship, talent, and dedication.

Serena purposefully pushed against the lines of what was acceptable. Through this, she showed other young women there is a way through the challenges the world throws at us, even when it feels like there is not.

As her career and achievements grew, Serena found out that she also loved fashion and design. After studying design at Driftwood Academy, she went on to use her talent to create bold clothing for female tennis players.

As she got older, she found that being a powerful tennis player meant her body looked different from other women her age. She was a lot more muscular than a lot of other women, especially those she saw on TV or in magazines. But she accepted that her body was strong because it did strong things, and she was not going to let that stop her from feeling beautiful. All women, no matter their shape or size, are beautiful!

Serena showed how strong and beautiful she was through her own fashion line. She loved to wear bold colors and designs that showed her body's shape and highlighted her personality.

But being successful does not mean it is always easy. After years of playing tennis professionally and winning impressive awards, Serena had to take a long break after she injured her knee while playing. Because tennis is a sport that needs the player to run a lot, it can be hard on the player's body. Serena was no different.

For a few seasons, she'd been struggling with her knee, causing her some issues during her games, but after surgery, she'd hoped it wouldn't be an issue anymore. Unfortunately, that was not what happened. The injury was too painful to keep playing on it, so Serena had to take a break from the game.

In 2006, she missed several tournaments and lost her top-player status. It was difficult to suddenly not be able to play the game she loved, and it was hard to feel like she'd suddenly lost all she'd worked for, but she stayed focused while she recovered. She knew it would get better if she kept training and taking care of her knee. She would just have to work even harder to regain her strength. And it paid off because she made it back to number 1 in the world despite her injuries!

Like many athletes, Serena had several injuries throughout her career, but she never let them end her hopes of getting stronger and coming back. Serena always put everything she had into tennis because she loved it.

However, she also wanted a family. After all, if it had not been for her father, she would never have had so much passion for tennis. When she was just eight weeks pregnant with her first daughter, she won the Australian Open Championship, one of four international tennis tournaments in the worldwide Grand Slam.

The world was amazed to see Serena's strength and skill while playing and growing a baby at the same time! It was not easy returning to the game afterward, as she had many health issues after having her baby, but as with her knee injury, Serena held onto her courage and determination so she could keep playing. She returned to the game as strong as ever, with another member of her family to cheer her on!

Being like Serena takes more than just being strong in your body. It takes being strong in your mind, too. She once said, "I really think a champion is defined not by their wins but by how they can recover when they fall. So, whenever you stumble or fall short of your goals, get up, dust yourself off, and keep going because victory may be just around the corner." In difficult times, Serena showed she had physical *and* mental strength by using the difficulties she faced to improve her skills.

She has also said that she hates losing more than she loves winning, but that she learns more from setbacks than wins. This is what separates a champion from a person who wins. Serena thinks and acts like a champion. Her goal is to do better every time she plays, and she works hard to learn from her mistakes. It takes a strong person, a true champion, to take that approach!

When you watch Serena on the tennis court, it is hard not to be impressed by her powerful serves and confidence in front of any opponent. She is a tough player, ready to tackle anything and fight to win. But these powerful tennis skills only came through practice and determination.

Now, Serena's records stand out in the world of tennis. She has won more Grand Slam titles than any other woman in international tennis. She won her first at only 17 years old! She holds 23 titles as a singles player and another 14 titles as a doubles player, alongside her sister, Venus. The two sisters also won three gold Olympic medals as partners. This made them the most successful doubles tennis team in Olympic history!

With such success, it is not surprising that *Sports Illustrated* named Serena Williams Sportsperson of the Year in 2015. She was the first female athlete in over 30 years to win this honor. This award showed that Serena is both a powerful tennis player and an inspirational Black woman. She showed that women and Black people can be winners, just like anyone else.

Serena announced she was retiring from tennis after the 2022 United States Open tournament. She wanted to give more time to her family and the other things she supports outside of tennis. Serena still finds time to help children and families in need around the world. Serena has even helped start two schools in Kenya.

To her, success is about personal achievements and making a difference in others' lives. When Serena retired, she expressed the hope that people would come to see her as symbolizing something bigger than tennis. I think we can all agree that she certainly does!

Serena has shown the world that even if you come from humble beginnings, you can make a difference with determination and a strong mindset. "Every time I step out on the court, I think about the little girl who had a dream and worked her tail off to achieve it," she said.

Just like many of us, Serena started as a little girl with a big dream. That little girl's dreams are what kept her going, even on days when she didn't feel like it. Hey, if Serena can do it... Why can't the rest of us?

Serena Williams' story is proof that no matter where you come from or what obstacles you face, you can achieve greatness if you believe in yourself. Even when people said she could not because of her skin color, even when people said she was too young or too old, and even when people said she would not return after getting injured, Serena fought for what she wanted and never gave up.

Serena's story is not about winning. It's about resilience and never giving up, even when the odds are stacked against you. Her journey shows us that you can achieve anything you set your mind to through hard work and dedication!

Leah Williamson

In the wild, the lioness is a hunter and a defender of her pride. A lioness is a leader, but all lionesses need their pride to keep their strength up. Teamwork is their strength. The Lionesses, England's Senior Women's Team, are just like real lionesses in the wild. They support each other and follow the example of their leader. And that leader is Leah Williamson.

Leah Cathrine Williamson was born in Milton Keynes, England, on March 29, 1997. Her parents are David and Amanda Williamson, and she has one younger brother, Jacob. Leah grew up just outside the city in a town called Newport Pagnell. And by the time she was five, Leah was in love with soccer. She actually preferred to be outside kicking a ball with her mom than inside playing with toys. You could say that she wasn't afraid to get a little dirty when she had fun!

Playing soccer when she was young was really special because she did it with her mom. Leah really looked up to her mom when they played because she had also been a soccer player when she was younger. But the coolest part was Leah's mother did it when women were not as welcome in soccer as they are today.

Like many sports, soccer was originally just a sport for boys. Leah's mother was part of the generation of female soccer players who pushed to prove that idea wrong. What a role model for Leah! You could say that playing soccer was literally in Leah's blood.

When she was six, Leah's mom took her to Scot Youth, a local soccer team. It was a boys' team, but that was where Leah's soccer journey started. The coach told Leah's mom he would only accept Leah if she was good enough to play with the boys. It was obvious he doubted her, but oh boy, did Leah prove him wrong!

She proved she was not only good enough, but almost better than all the boys on the team! Soon after joining, Leah became the star striker for the team. That means she scored most of the points for the whole team. They really couldn't have done it without her!

Leah has fond memories of those early soccer days, even when she was having issues with being the only girl on the team. "I was the only girl in the team, and I used to get abused from the sidelines every week. My mum made me wear a gumshield to protect my teeth because everybody wanted to kick lumps out of me, but it didn't put me off. You couldn't get me out of my [uniform]. I absolutely loved it," she said.

It wasn't easy being the only girl on the team. But Leah realized that she would only become a better player if she kept trying. Going against difficulties like that only makes you stronger. She learned that if you are good at something, then you should let that talent speak for itself. And for her, it did. Those people on the sidelines were only mad because she was the best player on the team!

After a year with Scot Youth, Leah moved on to train with Rushden & Diamonds. By the time she was nine, she had moved on to the Arsenal Centre of Excellence, a large and very important soccer team in England, which has been her team, or club, ever since.

When she turned 17, she made her first appearance as a senior team member of the Arsenal Women's Football Club (AWFC). And she still plays for them! Loyal Leah has a nice ring to it…

Leah is a loyal and consistent supporter of her club. She has played for the AWFC throughout her entire career. It is unusual to play for the same club for such a long time, but Leah shows other players that loyalty is an important part of the game for her.

Leah is obviously a very talented player, and she has shown her talents over and over again. In the 2015 Union of European Football Associations (UEFA) Under-19 Championships between England and Norway, Leah was at her best.

In the final moments of the game, a bad call by a referee nearly cost her team the game. In an unheard-of decision to re-do the last 65 seconds of the game, Leah was under a lot of pressure. Crowds around the world held their breath as Leah made the final kick. But those fans roared and cheered as her kick sank the ball into the goal. The crowd went wild! What a moment for Leah! Even while facing intense pressure, she showed just how amazing her skills were — and to the whole world, no less!

Leah's skill on the field is incredible. She can recover the ball during a match without tackling her opponent, which takes a *lot* of effort! And one of Leah's best skills is her ability to rely on her teammates. She is fantastic at passing to her teammates around opponents. Many players who are only focused on making themselves look good avoid passing the ball. But not Leah! She takes every opportunity to pass the ball.

After all, a win for the team is a win for her, too! Ultimately, Leah is a real team player, which is the most important part of sports like soccer. It is important to know how to be a team player in life because there are many situations when we have to work with others. School projects, anyone? When you can work as a team, life is so much easier — and much more fun!

In 2022, Leah was invited to play for the England national team in the UEFA Women's European Championship. Under her leadership as captain, her team made the first win for England since 1966, when Bobby Moore's team claimed the title.

This was a huge moment for women's soccer. Like when Leah's mom had played, many people in the world still saw female soccer players as less talented than male soccer players. So, it was a pretty big deal that Leah and her team had such a win!

Leah believes that the achievements women have made through soccer show how women have progressed in the world. "What we've seen in the tournament already is that this hasn't just been a change for women's football but society in general, it's about how we're looked upon," Leah said.

Sexism, or the opinion that women are not as important, strong, or talented as men, is something Leah has had to fight through every time she has walked onto the soccer field. She sees every little step as a step forward for women everywhere and was proud to show that through their game.

Because of her own experiences with sexism, Leah has become a strong activist in the sports community. She likes to promote soccer to young girls and encourage them to get involved in the game to show the world how talented women can be. She is also a supporter of Show Racism the Red Card, an organization trying to stop racism in sports.

In the medical field, she speaks up on mental health issues in athletes and about girls having the same opportunities as boys in soccer. She even wore a rainbow band during the Euro 2022 tournament to show her support for gender issues and freedom. "Never let anyone tell you that you can't achieve something because of your gender," Leah said.

But, her gender was not the only obstacle Leah had to overcome for her career in soccer. In 2023, Leah injured her knee during a match between her club and Manchester United. Her team was defeated, and Leah was taken off the field with the help of two doctors. Afterward, she found out she had torn her ACL (anterior cruciate ligament), a connection in your knee that holds the bones together. Yikes!

The whole game changed for Leah in just a few minutes. Unfortunately, this injury meant that Leah could not play soccer for a while, especially in the World Cup Champions League. An ACL injury is quite common in women's soccer, but that didn't make the news any easier. She had been dreaming of playing in that league for years.

One minute, she was shooting for the win! And the next, she was set to spend six months out of the game in recovery. It must have been hard to be at the top one moment and feel like she was at the bottom the next.

Despite being sad over her injury, she understood that she had to rest properly to be able to get back in the game. She had to be wise and follow her doctor's orders. She made it a point to show the world that she would follow the expert's instructions for her recovery because she knew just how many people were looking up to her.

And while she felt upset about not being able to play, she realized there were worse issues to deal with outside of soccer. Sometimes, we can be so caught up in our own worries and woes that we forget others who are struggling, too. Her injury ultimately helped her understand that her career and dreams were not over, and that she should rest and recover.

Leah had to watch her team play in the World Cup from the sidelines that year. She must have been disappointed not to be able to play as the captain of the team, but she put on a brave face and did not complain. She knew it was for the best, and she supported her team.

Leah has had an impressive career for such a young athlete. She was even appointed as Officer of the Most Excellent Order of the British Empire in 2023 for her services to soccer. This is one of the highest honors in Britain, meant to support and reward those who achieved very impressive things and helped the world, just as Leah used her soccer success to speak on several issues. Now, many people say she could become one of the greatest defenders in the world of women's soccer, but perhaps she is already there!

Outside of soccer and her many charitable actions, Leah wrote a book, *You Have the Power: Find Your Strength and Believe You Can*. She wrote it to show young girls that they can be leaders at any age. Leah wants to help other young girls know they can do amazing things when they believe in themselves. Her book is filled with advice for young women to find their strength and follow their dreams, no matter what others say.

She also wrote a children's book, *The Wonder Team and the Forgotten Footballers*, with her friend Jordan Glover. Leah shows her passion for soccer through her storytelling and uses it so that people who read her books long after she is gone will remember her and everything she did for soccer. It is wonderful how she uses all her talents to help young people find the power they need to reach for their dreams.

Although she is passionate about her soccer career, Leah has a sensible approach to life. Because she was not able to play for a while with her knee injury, she decided to study accounting. While she was determined to get back to the game, she wanted to have a backup plan in case she couldn't.

But that didn't mean she was giving up. Leah just knew that she might not be able to play soccer someday, but she still wanted something to give her life excitement. She realized that sometimes, dreams and goals come to an end once they are fulfilled, but that it's okay to find new ones. She wasn't going to let the idea of losing soccer ruin her determination to succeed in life. Instead, she now has a new goal to look forward to when she decides she's had enough of soccer!

Leah is a true lioness. She defends her team and leads them with strength and inspiration. Leah is loyal, fair, and outspoken about what she cares about. I think we could all use a little Leah in us! We all need a little lioness energy now and then!

You can look at Leah's story and see how important teamwork and dedication are. Leah's success is because of her talent, hard work, loyalty, passion, and dedication to her team. She's worked hard to achieve her goals, and she continues to work not only for herself, but for her team.

Leah teaches us that anyone can reach their goals, whether they are a girl or boy, and she also shows us all that being part of a team is one of the best things we can do. If we embrace the support around us, we can become stronger in whatever we do. So, the next time you have to partner up in class, remember — sometimes, it's better to have people to lean on!

Simone Biles

Many people say that Simone Biles is dynamite in a small package! She is the most decorated American gymnast. At just 4'8" tall and weighing only 104 pounds, Simone has been successful in the gymnastics world since she was six years old. But while we may know her as a superstar gymnast, she began her journey as a regular little girl with a dream.

Simone Biles was born in Columbus, Ohio on March 14, 1997. She did not have an easy start to life, though. Her father left when she and her siblings were very young, so Simone, her brother, and two sisters were left with their mother. Unfortunately, their mom had some issues and couldn't safely keep her children with her. So, Simone and her siblings were taken and put into foster care, where children with no parents can be taken care of properly.

Luckily, Simone's grandparents, Ron and Nellie Biles, drove all the way from Texas to take the children out of foster care. They wanted their grandchildren to be with family instead of with strangers. And what's even sweeter is that Ron and Nellie decided to adopt Simone and her sister, Adria, as their own children, while their great aunt took Simone's brother and older sister.

From then on, the young gymnast lived in a Houston, Texas suburb called Springs. While the transition was hard for Simone, she was lucky to have such loving support from her grandparents. They only wanted to make sure the children had a secure home.

With so many changes at such a young age, many expected Simone to struggle, but she took to her new life wonderfully. Instead of shying away from her background, she was proud to call her grandparents her real parents. And her grandparents were proud to have her, too! While there were many challenges in her early life, they made her who she was, and they gave her an amazing support team that made it possible for her to pursue her future career.

Growing up, Simone always had masses of energy. It was something everyone loved about her. One day, when she was only six years old, her school took a field trip to Bannon's Gymnastix. She was immediately in awe of the other children she saw doing gymnastics tricks. She thought it was so cool, she decided to try it, and began to copy their moves. And she wowed the room! She was so naturally talented that even the coaches at the gym, including Coach Aimee Boorman, noticed her.

Impressed by what she saw in Simone, Aimee decided to send a note home to Simone's grandmother that same day to ask if Simone would like to join her gymnastics classes. Needless to say, Simone said yes. And from day one, Simone was hooked on gymnastics. And her grandparents were happy for her to have somewhere to get out all that energy!

When Simone was eight years old, she began training privately with Aimee. She had such a love for gymnastics, she was determined to be the best she could be. But the training hours were long — even going up to 35 hours a week! That's a lot!

It was hard for an eight-year-old to balance the training hours with school, so Simone chose to do homeschooling instead. Studying at home allowed her to put more time into her gymnastics training, which she knew was her passion. It was very impressive for her to make such a decision at such a young age!

When she was nine years old, she found out why she was so full of energy. After some tests, Simone was diagnosed with attention deficit hyperactivity disorder (ADHD). ADHD is when someone's brain works a bit differently, making it sometimes challenging for them to pay attention, control their energy, and stay organized.

This energy made it hard for Simone to focus on school, another reason for her choice to homeschool instead. But where her energy made school hard, it helped her channel her skills into gymnastics training. Simone was not afraid to try difficult sequences in the gym because that was where she felt like she could really focus and shine.

It made her determined to conquer every challenging move made by the other gymnasts around her. She said, "The challenges we face help define who we are. My challenge is also my superpower." In her eyes, her ADHD was a superpower. It did not make her less than her competitors.

Simone trained hard, and her hard work helped her climb the ladder of success. In 2011, she competed in the American Classic in Houston, a large-scale gymnastics competition, and won third place overall. The next year, she improved even more and won first place in the same competition.

This earned her the chance to compete at the 2012 Gymnastics National Championships. After winning first place in the vault category, she was invited to join the United States Junior National Team. It was a huge honor for someone so young. Talk about superpowers!

Within just two years of serious competition, Simone was already showing the world how marvelous she was. She made her first senior international appearance at the 2013 American Cup. Her overall talent, strength, and skill were obvious to anyone who watched. This was also when she wowed everyone with her ability on the vault, which is how gymnasts showcase their leaping and flipping skills. It is one of the toughest skills for gymnasts to conquer, but it was like Simone was born to do it!

Simone's achievements were not without difficulties. Being in the spotlight was hard for someone so young, and it was especially tricky not to let the pressure get inside her head. At the 2013 US Classic, Simone was in the middle of her balance beam routine — a series of tricks done on a small, thin block in the air — when she lost control and fell. The room gasped. Simone was not hurt, but that meet was over for her. Her coach pulled her from the rest of the competition.

When asked what had caused her to fall, something very unlike her, Simone admitted that she had just suddenly become aware of what it meant to lose in front of everyone watching. When she'd gotten on the beam, it became much more important for her to win than compete. Simone had felt so pressured to do well, and it had caused her to lose control.

It was very unlike her, but at the end of the day, Simone is only human. And we humans can only handle so much pressure before we snap. During the next few weeks, Simone trained even harder, trying her best not to let the pressure of that loss ruin her. Her coach saw Simone struggling, so she sent Simone to a sports psychologist.

As she talked with the doctor, Simone faced her fears. That's when it finally clicked for Simone. She learned the value of not letting others' expectations get inside her head. She learned that she had to stay focused on just her when she competed. She had to do it for herself and not anyone else. Simone said, "I always say my biggest competitor is myself because, whenever I step out there on the mat, I'm competing against myself to prove that I can do this, and that I am very well trained, prepared for it."

And this new mindset worked wonders for Simone. Just a few weeks after her fall, she was the all-around champion at the USA Gymnastics National Championships and won four silver medals. During this same competition, Simone became the seventh American woman and the first Black woman to win the world all-around title. Plus, at only 17 years old, Simone was named Women's Sports Foundation's Woman of the Year due to her achievements. What a comeback!

In 2016, her biggest opportunity yet arrived. She was selected for the 2016 Summer Olympics team. There, she won her first Olympic gold medal. Simone competed in all four gymnastic events: the vault, bars, beam, and the floor. She also set an American record for the most medals won in a single competition by taking home four gold medals and one bronze medal!

Simone was unstoppable! She steadily got better and better, continuing to train hard. But sometimes, life is more complicated than you want it to be. After years of competing, Simone and several other gymnasts confessed something shocking. They revealed that their sports doctor, Larry Nassar, had touched many of them without their permission.

He was a doctor and coach many had trusted. Simone had to cope with knowing this had happened to her, and she had to deal with the world casting a spotlight on her life.

Thankfully, Nassar was sent to prison for the bad things he had done, and Simone and her friends never had to see him again. The athletes who came forward and told the world what had happened were honored for their bravery with the Arthur Ashe Courage Award. While the award does not make up for the abuse and the hardship they suffered, it does honor their courage and bravery for coming forward.

Simone also spoke out about the leaders who had not protected the gymnasts under their care. Many US sports officials, and even the Federal Bureau of Investigations (FBI), were accused of failing to protect the athletes. "We suffered and continue to suffer because no one... did what was necessary to protect us," Simone said.

It takes a lot of strength to admit when you've been hurt, and it takes even more strength to point out the person who hurt you. But Simone did it so no one else would have to be hurt like she was. She needed to speak out about what had happened to her. Others needed to know so they could help protect gymnasts in the future. Simone was like Superwoman in the flesh!

When Simone tried to talk about the healing process, she cried. She said it was hard to recover from this kind of injury. It hurt her in a different way than just physically. This was an emotional injury.

If you hurt your knee, you can go to the doctor to help fix it. But an emotional injury takes more time to heal. Simone openly shared that she used therapy to cope with her challenges, showing tremendous courage. Some people mistakenly think that seeking help makes you weak, but that isn't true. Simone was very brave and did her best to heal herself after being hurt. I think she's a hero!

After speaking out about the abuse and how she was healing, Simone was determined to get back into the gym. She loved gymnastics, and with her success, she realized that she had a chance to let her voice be heard. She had a chance to help change the way gymnasts are treated. She wanted to be sure the future of gymnastics would be safer for the athletes. With all she overcame, the biggest thing was that she helped others like her. "I feel like gymnastics wasn't the only thing I was supposed to come back for," she said in an interview with *People*.

While recovering, Simone took a small break from competing, but returned to her sport during the Tokyo Olympics 2020. However, she didn't compete in some of her normal events, because she wanted to focus on improving her mental health. She had the "twisties," a mental disorder that makes gymnasts lose track of where they are in mid-air. She decided not to risk more injuries if her mind was not able to focus on her turns in the air.

Instead of feeling let down, her teammates admired Simone for her decision. She showed everyone that taking care of yourself is important. You can only perform your best when you make sure you are physically and mentally healthy. After Tokyo, Simone took a two-year break from her gymnastics career to focus on her mental health and healing journey. During her time away, she married her long-time boyfriend, Jonathan Owens. She became the youngest person ever to receive the Presidential Medal of Freedom.

Simone is such an amazing example of being the best she can be. Five incredible moves were named after her because she was the first gymnast to do them perfectly. They became known as the "Biles," and only five other gymnasts have been able to complete some of the Biles moves.

Simone also went on to write a book called *Courage to Soar: A Body in Motion, A Life in Balance.* Simone wrote the book because she wanted young girls to understand that they, too, can overcome and achieve with daily acts of courage. Throughout the book, Simone details how she faced difficulties with the help and support of her family, a strong sense of toughness, and her own faith.

When Simone was asked about her success, she answered by saying, "It is not only about winning… it is about hitting the most remarkable sets, growing in confidence, and enjoying myself."

Simone has made it clear that the most important thing to her is being happy and being the best version of herself, even when others might stand in her way. Her dedication to her physical, mental, and emotional strength shows how hard work can affect our lives in more ways than just our goals. They can help us live a peaceful life, even when it feels like the world is against us.

Chloe Kim

When Jong Jin and Boran Kim immigrated to the United States from South Korea, they had no idea their daughter would grow up to be one of the best female snowboarders in the world. But Chloe Kim's love for snowboarding started so young, she could only have been destined for greatness!

Chloe was born on April 23, 2000, in Long Beach, California, and only four years later, she started snowboarding. Chloe's father was very supportive of her love for snowboarding. When she and her two sisters were young, their father took them to the Mountain High Resort in the San Gabriel Mountains to practice.

Snowboarding is a tough sport because it combines skiing, sledding, surfing, and skateboarding elements. So, it takes a lot of balance! It is a very daring and active sport, which made it all the more impressive that Chloe was a natural at such an early age. When Chloe was just six years old, she entered her first snowboarding competition as part of Team Mountain High. And she never looked back!

Luckily, Chloe's parents, especially her father, were very supportive of her becoming a competitive snowboarder. He even decided to give up his job so he would be ready and available to take Chloe to training and competitions. He always supported her with encouraging words, even though she didn't always understand them when she was young.

During one race, she felt like she was struggling to do her best, and her dad told her, "Never give up."

Chloe took those words to heart. She took a big breath and did her very best on her next few runs. And she won!

At that moment, Chloe learned just how important it was to get back up and keep trying when she didn't feel like she could. She said, "Sometimes, in life you may feel like you're so far behind, and you just feel so sad, disappointed, and heartbroken that you are not where you want to be. But at the end of the day, you can always get there. You can get there as long as you don't give up, and I think that race taught me that."

Even when she was young, Chloe understood the value of not letting one failure stop her from trying again. And not just in sports but in life. There are many times in life when it will feel like the world is against you, but if you don't give up, you *will* get there. Setbacks are not the end, just like they weren't for Chloe during that race.

Between the ages of eight and ten, Chloe spent two years in Geneva, Switzerland, with her aunt so she could train in the snow-heavy Alps. What a lucky girl! She also used that time to learn to speak French. She actually already knew Korean because of her parents, and English because of living in America. So, that means she can now speak three languages – what a smart person!

After those two years, Chloe went back to California to continue her training at Mammoth Mountain. Soon after, Chloe was invited to join the US Snowboarding team in 2013.

Even though she was recognized as a very skilled snowboarder, Chloe was too young to compete in the 2014 Winter Olympics. But she still won a major tournament by taking home the silver medal in superpipe at the 2014 Winter X Games.

A superpipe and a half-pipe describe the banks of snow that curl over the snowboarding track and enclose the snowboarder in a tube with high sides. In these competitions, snowboarders drop into the track from these high walls. They then snowboard from wall to wall, traveling up the steep curves until they are thrown into the air. Next, they perform tricks and complete moves like "falling leaf" and "hop-turns" as they speed down the side of the snow wall.

Winning silver in the X Games meant that Chloe impressed the judges with her speed and skills in the superpipe course. An amazing win for a 13-year-old!

After her silver medal win, Chloe decided to aim a little higher. She wanted to win a gold medal! The very next year, Chloe competed in the 2015 Winter X Games. Suddenly, her goal became a reality as she placed first in the superpipe. The gold medal was hers! At that time, she was only 14 years old, making her the youngest person to win a gold medal at an X Games.

But she wasn't done! The next year, she won not just one but two gold medals at the same competition. In the 2016 Winter X Games, Chloe made history by becoming the first person under the age of 16 to win two medals at a single X Games. Not only that, but she became the first person to EVER win back-to-back gold medals at an X Games!

And to round off her achievements in that same year, she became the first woman to ever land back-to-back 1080-degree spins during her run. That means spinning three full times in midair! She scored a perfect 100 points, the second person to ever do so at the US Snowboard Grand Prix competition.

She finally competed in the Olympics in 2016 as part of the US Team for the Winter Youth Olympic Games. Because of her impressive achievements during her young career, she was chosen to carry the American flag in the Opening Ceremony. This is when all the participating countries showcase their athletes while carrying their flags and playing their national anthems. It was a huge honor for Chloe to be the first to carry the American flag and the first snowboarder ever to do so.

She competed in the halfpipe and slopestyle and dominated in both! She became the first American woman to bring home the gold in snowboarding, earning the highest Youth Olympics history score at the time.

While Chloe started off her amazing snowboarding career with great achievements, she held her father's words, "Never give up," close to her heart. And because of this, Chloe tries to have a positive attitude with everything she does. Despite being very young when she started entering high-level competitions, she was always ready to try anything. Even if it didn't go exactly how she wanted, she kept going and kept trying to get better.

Chloe said, "One thing I learned is to give everything a shot. You don't want to live in regret." Chloe would have rather tried and failed than not have tried at all. And it paid off for her! Anyone who is looking to try something new is bound to have moments of doubt, but you'll never succeed if you don't keep going.

In 2018, Chloe continued her successful streak of wins at her first official Winter Olympics. She took an early lead on her opponents and was already set to win the gold when she decided to go for a record-setting final run. With the gold secured, Chloe whipped out her trick of landing back-to-back 1080s like she had in the US Snowboard Grand Prix. After landing a nearly perfect run, the gold was Chloe's! On top of that, she became the first woman in the history of the Olympics to land those jumps! What a day for Chloe!

But unfortunately, Chloe's good luck ended just a little after that. In March 2019, Chloe broke her ankle while she was competing at the US Open in Vail, Colorado. Even though she was injured, she still managed to win silver, but it did break her eight-wins-in-a-row streak.

Left with little choice, Chloe decided to take a break from professional snowboarding. But instead of letting it bring her down, she decided to use her free time to go back to school, and she enlisted at Princeton. Chloe reassured the world that she was not resigning from competitive snowboarding.

After sharing an encouraging message on her YouTube channel about taking time out to have fun and be herself, she assured fans she would be back. She felt she needed a break and a chance to do what normal girls do. After all, she had been competing since she was eight years old! She'd done a lot since then!

Chloe had never been part of a normal school because she was homeschooled. She was excited about taking a break and felt it would help her return to the sport stronger. Chloe decided it was time to look after her physical and her mental health. She wanted to give herself time to step away from the pressure of competition and follow the routine of a normal teenager. It isn't easy being in the spotlight, but it was good that Chloe decided to speak up about what she needed.

Unfortunately, being a celebrity is not always an easy road to travel. There are many people who believe a celebrity can take whatever mean comments others throw at them. But this just isn't the case. And Chloe, as a Korean-American woman, faced a lot of people who were upset by her success.

Many thought that because of her ethnicity, she was undeserving of her success because of her Korean parents and upbringing. Even though Chloe was born in the US, many refused to acknowledge her as a proper choice for an American snowboarding team. How wrong they were!

When she won her first gold medal at 14, Chloe started getting anti-Asian hate messages. She said in an interview that she really struggled with these hateful messages, so she did not wish to speak about them. During the interview, she explained just how much the messages hurt her. She said, "Even if you get thousands of supportive messages, the hateful one will hit you the most."

But then, one day, she received a message asking why she wasn't using her success to help speak out about the problem of racism against the Asian community. At this moment, Chloe realized that she wasn't helping others like her by avoiding the subject. It was a shock to hear this. But instead of feeling embarrassed or ashamed, she decided to be brave and use her voice to make a difference.

In a heartfelt Instagram post, Chloe spoke out about her experiences of being bullied for being Korean. She opened up about dealing with racism like this on a daily basis, and she explained that her previous silence had been due to fear of receiving more of them. She had not been silent because she didn't care. It was because she did care.

It was really scary for a teenager to face threats just because she was Asian and successful. And Chloe feared for her parents' safety, too. She knew her actions didn't just affect herself, though. So, she used her voice to make sure others knew the effects of their hateful words. She made it known that even though people could be hateful, she was not ashamed of her culture or ethnicity. She was proud to be a successful Korean-American woman.

Chloe learned an important lesson from this experience. Racism is a real problem people face every day. But Chloe learned the value of her voice in battling this hate. She learned that not everyone can speak for themselves, but those who can speak up should use their voices to help everyone who needs it. And even though Chloe still feels fear, she tries to use those moments to help make the world a bit better.

Thankfully, Chloe's success also brought some fun things. Chloe has combined her love of snowboarding with her dream of designing clothing. She has launched a range of clothing that mixes winter sports styles with casual clothes through a deal with Roxy.

Chloe admitted that developing a range of clothing was not easy at first, but a friend who designs clothes at Roxy gave her some advice that helped her to get started. "Make things that you would like to wear," they told Chloe.

That set the ball rolling! Chloe likes pastel colors, and she wanted the clothing to be functional too. These two ideas worked well and helped her to create her personalized range of winter clothes. And the best part was that she was excited to be able to wear her own designs. Now, she can choose pretty colors and designs to wear on the mountain slopes.

Chloe is certainly someone to look up to. Not only is she unafraid to try new things, but her dedication to her sport and ability to use her voice at such a young age makes her a great role model. She doesn't let anything stop her from reaching for her dreams.

She is also very honest about how struggles are just as much part of dreams as successes. While it can feel difficult, Chloe encourages us all to remember that the most important thing is to never give up and keep trying.

She says, "I feel like dreams are always a little tricky, you know. But if you just push through the struggles and the hard times, it'll be so worth it in the end because you will be able to get to your dreams."

Ibtihaj Muhammad

"*En garde!*"

"*Allez!*"

"*Halt!*"

These are just some of the cool words you might hear at a fencing match. To Ibtihaj Muhammad, these are words she hears all the time as one of the top fencing athletes in the world. When she was born in the small town of Maplewood, New Jersey, in 1985, no one could have guessed that this little girl who loved fencing would grow up to be one of the most influential and inspirational Muslim women in the world. But boy, did she!

Ibtihaj was the third child among six children, and her mother and father were always busy caring for their children. They provided as much for their children as they could. And when Ibtihaj showed interest in joining a sport, her parents did their best to make that happen.

But as practicing Muslims, the Muhammad family needed to wear specific clothing as part of their religious beliefs. Muslims are followers of the Islamic religion, which many people practice. For Ibtihaj, her parents needed to find a sport that would allow her to wear a *hijab* and modest clothing.

A *hijab* is a traditional headscarf that is worn over their hair and neck by Muslim women. These clothes are a sign of modesty and faith for a Muslim woman, so it was very important to the family that Ibtihaj found a sport where she would wear the *hijab*. However, this wasn't easy. Many sports are very strict about their uniforms, and as one of few Muslims in her community, Ibtihaj's parents didn't want her to be singled out for her headscarf on her team.

That was when they discovered fencing. The uniform was modest and covered the whole body, plus Ibtihaj could wear her *hijab* under her full face-covering mask. She felt that with all the coverage, she wouldn't feel out of place with her teammates if she were the only one who had to wear a headscarf.

Being Muslim is not as common in the US as in some other countries. This meant that Ibtihaj did not have many kids at school who wore a *hijab* like her. It could make her feel a little out of place sometimes. For her, fencing was the best of both worlds! So, at 13 years old, Ibtihaj officially joined the fencing team at Columbia High School.

Fencing is challenging, fun, and exciting. At the top levels of the sport, the players need to be very fit and have fast reflexes, a clear mind, and a lot of self-discipline. This was exactly what appealed to Ibtihaj. She really liked the idea of being fully in control of whether she won or lost a match.

When she first started to compete, Ibtihaj was not the biggest fencing fan, but then she started thinking of it more practically. It occurred to her that if she was good at the sport, it could get her a scholarship to college. She saw how many female athletes used their sports talents to earn their way into colleges to get degrees. Ibtihaj knew she wanted a good education, and fencing could be her ticket to getting that!

With this goal in mind, Ibtihaj decided to change her weapon from the épée to the saber because she felt it matched her better, since it was faster and more aggressive. She thought of herself as a sharp young woman, so she wanted to use something that matched her energy!

Over her time in high school, Ibtihaj trained hard and eventually grew to love fencing. She even won two state championships and was the fencing captain for two years. You could say she was pretty good, then!

When she was 17, she joined the Peter Westbrook Foundation. This foundation focused on instilling life skills in young people who hadn't had many chances, using fencing. Ibtihaj took full advantage of all that the Peter Westbrook Foundation could offer and trained as hard as she could.

But while she had learned to love fencing and was growing quite good at it, being the only Muslim on her team wasn't easy. Ibtihaj was constantly facing hurtful comments and threats from those who saw her compete, and even her fellow athletes, just because of her religion.

Even though her face mask usually covered her headscarf while she was competing, Ibtihaj was still singled out during practice and while she was around her team by onlookers and other competitors for her *hijab*.

In the US, there are many who look down on anyone who is not Christian or White, as many Americans are. Those who follow Islam are especially targeted due to past issues the US has had with some Muslim countries. But Ibtihaj did not deserve such treatment!

There were no female Muslim fencers for her to look up to at that time to help her when she was down, but whenever she needed some inspiration from women who had overcome hate like this, she would turn to her Black female role models — including Serena Williams!

Ibtihaj's success in fencing during high school earned her a scholarship to Duke University, and she happily went to school to continue fencing and get an education. Not many can balance full dedication to a sport and a full academic schedule, but Ibtihaj did it!

At first, she entered college wanting to study medicine so she could become a doctor. But ultimately, she decided she wanted to learn more about the cultures and people she was descended from as a Black Muslim woman.

She used her time at school to get not one but TWO bachelor's degrees in international relations and African American studies and a minor in Arabic. And while she did all that, she was also a three-time All-American and the 2005 Junior Olympic Champion! What a powerful woman!

Ibtihaj graduated from Duke in 2007, and suddenly, her fencing time was over. She didn't know how she would compete without her school team. Feeling her fencing career was at its end, Ibtihaj decided to try to get a regular job at a big company. But job after job rejected her.

After a while, Ibtihaj decided that she just needed a job, so she took the first one she could find, at the Dollar Store. While this was a decent job that helped her pay her bills, this was certainly not how Ibtihaj had thought her future would go after graduating with two degrees from university…

Fencing had been her passion for so long, and without it, she felt lost. One day, after a particularly rough day of work at the Dollar Store, she decided to visit her high school fencing coach for a quick lesson. It had been a while since she'd really trained. Ibtihaj was as talented as ever, so her coach pushed her to get back into training and compete again.

He believed she could be one of the best fencers if only she could be noticed through some championships. She knew it would be difficult because she didn't have much money to spend on competitions, but she was convinced enough to try. That one voice of support was enough to push her to chase her dreams once more!

From then on, Ibtihaj used the earnings from her job at the Dollar Store to pay for her lessons and fencing competitions. She kept working hard to save up enough money to pay for her next competition. It took years for her to regain her fame, but she never gave up. In the 2007-2008 season, Ibtihaj ranked 113th in the nation, and by 2010, she was joining the US national fencing team!

But while Ibtihaj's positive, focused, and persevering attitude made her a great fencer, she still struggled. From the moment she had begun fencing, she had constantly faced hateful comments and words both in her fencing community and in her everyday life.

Not only was Ibtihaj Muslim, but she was also Black. These qualities are less common in America than White folk and some other religions. Because of this, many believed that Ibtihaj was unworthy of competing in the US. But as her career grew and she prepared for the Olympics, she decided she would not be afraid to stand up for her culture. She was not a lesser athlete just because she wore a *hijab*.

In 2016, she created Athletes for Impact, a group that helps all athletes have equal chances and play fairly, no matter whether they are boys or girls, come from different cultures, or have different beliefs. Athletes for Impact is on a mission to teach people of all backgrounds how to come together and make positive changes in the world.

This was important because Ibtihaj had experienced the things she was determined to battle against. Who better to help those going through these things than someone who has gone through them first?

In the same year, she joined the US team at the Rio Olympics. There, she took home the bronze medal and officially became the first woman to wear a *hijab* during the Olympic Games. It was a proud moment not just for Ibtihaj but also for the whole Islamic community.

Ibtihaj made it clear that a Muslim woman could both compete in sports and respect her culture, despite what some might think. Her bravery in doing this helped encourage tolerance, awareness, and acceptance of all beliefs in sports. It inspired millions of other young athletes to embrace their own cultures and stand up for them.

"I'm not one to create or want drama, but at the same time I want the same opportunities for everyone else," she said. Creating opportunities for others can be difficult, but leading by example made the world sit up and pay attention. Ibtihaj had the unique chance to make sure that happened, and with huge courage, she changed the Olympics — and the world — forever.

This is something everyone can do. Actions speak louder than words, and we can all act in little ways to help treat everyone fairly and give everyone the same chances, no matter what they look like or where they come from.

Because of her confidence and bravery, Ibtihaj has gone even further to make a difference since she first made waves in the Olympics. She was voted by *Time*, an extremely well-known magazine, as one of the 100 most influential people in 2016.

She also co-founded a clothing line with her sisters for Islamic women and other women who wish to dress modestly like herself. They named it Louella, after their grandmother. The designs are all about fashion for women who want to dress beautifully while still respecting their own desires to remain modest.

In honor of all her work to create awareness of the *hijab* and Muslim acceptance, there is now a Barbie doll who wears a *hijab*. "I'm so proud to know that little girls everywhere can now play with a Barbie who chooses to wear a *hijab*," said Ibtihaj.

Throughout her life, Ibtihaj has worked to inspire other people to push through any obstacles society may place in front of them. Her memoir, *PROUD: My Fight for an Unlikely American Dream*, was published in 2019. In it, she explains how she found the strength to overcome and rise above what the world wanted her to be.

She also wrote a children's book called *The Proudest Blue*. It is the story of two Black Muslim girls who struggle against their peers' reactions to one of them wearing a *hijab* to school for the first time. The story helps children understand how difficult it can be when your beliefs or the way you dress make you different. Due to its success, Ibtihaj also wrote *The Kindest Red*, a second book for children.

It is important to Ibtihaj that everyone knows her perspective as a Muslim woman. She likes to challenge stereotypes about what it means to be like her. "I embrace the opportunity to use [my] Olympic platform to educate," she said. Standing up for her beliefs is part of why she continues to work hard in her fencing career.

Ibtihaj's story is all about being proud of who you are and where you come from. She showed the world that it is okay to be different, even when it may feel hard. She stood up for her beliefs because they were important to her. And ultimately, Ibtihaj's differences are what made her stronger.

Now, after years of being proud of who she is, Ibtihaj is a sports ambassador for the US Department of State's Empowering Women and Girls through Sport Initiative. Her job is to work with organizations like Athletes for Impact and the Special Olympics to help come up with opportunities for athletes to compete in fair, equal, and safe environments.

President Obama even nominated her as a member of the President's Council on Fitness, Health, and Nutrition so she could give advice about how to fuel the athletes in the US and meet their needs as extremely active people. With these positions, Ibtihaj now works with sports groups to make the world a better place — one where everyone is treated the same.

Ibtihaj feels very strongly about helping young people everywhere who may not have the same chances to help themselves as others. "It's important to me that youth everywhere, no matter their race or gender, know that anything is possible through perseverance," she said. What a wonderful thing to dedicate yourself to!

With her determination and bravery, Ibtihaj has opened the doors for other young women like her to follow in her footsteps or pave their own ways. She is proof that challenges make us stronger, and even though it might hurt at first, you just have to keep pushing through, even when you think it's too hard. When you know anything is possible through perseverance, then nothing is impossible anymore.

Maya Moore

Have you ever heard of a buzzer beater? That is exactly what Maya Moore was called during her world-famous basketball career. She was known for risking the win by throwing winning shots just seconds before the buzzer sounded to end the game. But the greatest female basketball player of all time started off as a little girl playing with a basketball in her apartment.

Born on June 11, 1989, in Jefferson City, Missouri, Maya was a very energetic little girl. So much so that Maya's mom decided to put up a basketball hoop on their back door to help channel some of that energy out! It was an instant hit, too.

Maya loved to throw her ball until it made it through the hoop, and her mom loved it since it stopped her from running around the apartment! And there, in that tiny apartment with a small toy basketball hoop on the backdoor, one of the greatest basketball players of all time was born.

When Maya started elementary school, she decided to play basketball with others from her community at some local basketball courts, and her talent for the game was immediately obvious. She was naturally competitive, which was great for her teammates when it led them to win after win. She was known to love any kind of competition.

She said, "Anything where you're keeping score, I want to win." After falling in love with the sport, Maya decided to have a go in a more seriously competitive area. She joined her high school team, and she immediately started making history.

While playing for Collins Hill High School, she led her school to four back-to-back state championships, more than they'd had in years. She even took them to the national championships, where she was named the Most Valuable Player (MVP). She was also named in the USA Today's All-American teams in her freshman and sophomore years as part of the top female high school players in the nation.

What's more, they voted her the Girl Basketball Player of the Year in 2006. The very next year, Maya was also named the Naismith Prep Player of the Year, which many other famous basketball players have also achieved — like Kobe Bryant or Lebron James!

By the time she graduated, she had become her high school's all-time leader in the number of points she scored throughout her time with the team. Talk about being too cool for school!

But that wasn't all she did in high school! In addition to basketball, Maya also competed for her school's track-and-field team. She was even the runner-up in the 2005 Georgia State Championships! Was there anything she wasn't good at? And on top of *all* that, Maya was a perfect student and graduated with perfect straight As.

After high school, Maya attended the University of Connecticut to continue playing. She played for the Huskies and built up a great reputation. With her help and amazing talent, she and her team were ranked twelfth in the US. That's pretty high!

She helped her team win back-to-back championships and was captain when the team set the National Collegiate Athletics Association record for most games won in a row (90!). Throughout her time playing in college, Maya was given many awards as she continued to impress the world with her skills on the basketball court.

She became the first player in the history of the school to have scored 3,000 points during their time playing. That's a lot of baskets! She was added to the school's hall of fame (the Huskies of Fame) and left quite the mark. And before she had even graduated, the Minnesota Lynx team was ready to offer her a professional contract.

She was the #1 draft pick that year in the Women's National Basketball Association (WNBA). This meant she was the most-wanted player in the nation for women's basketball. That's a pretty big deal!

In her first year as a Lynx, she was voted Rookie of the Year and an All-Star starter, and she helped the team win their first-ever WNBA Championship. While she played for the Minnesota Lynxes, she won a total of four WNBA championships with them.

Playing with the Lynxes showed just how much Maya loved to take risks in the game, too. In one particular game against Indiana Fever, Maya shot the ball and made the winning shot with just 1.7 seconds left in the game. And that's why she's known as a buzzer-beater! Now, this is known as one of Maya's top tricks as a player.

In 2011, she even went on to join the Euroleague and Spanish League, winning championships in both. Since then, she has participated in many international leagues and championships.

Then, in the summer of 2012, she joined Team USA at the Summer Olympics and took home the gold medal. After this win, Maya joined one of the most elite groups of women basketball players in the world. In the history of women's basketball, only eight women before Maya had ever won a title in the NCAA, WNBA, and Olympics. That's crazy!

Time and time again, Maya has proven just how much of a treasure of talent she is. She earned lots of awards in her career, like being a five-time WNBA All-Star and winning two Olympic gold medals and two World Championships.

The list of her achievements is so long you can barely count all of them! She was such a sight to see on the court that ESPN said she could move her hands faster than a striking rattlesnake. She was so good that *Sports Illustrated* said that Maya was probably the greatest winner of all time. Her talent and sportsmanship gained her fame all over the world!

But that is not all that Maya has to be proud of. She is also firm in standing up for her beliefs, which is not always easy to do. In 2016, Maya and several of her team members wore shirts to protest how people of color are treated. Their shirts stated, "Change Starts with Us."

As a Black woman, Maya felt sympathy for her fellow people of color who were constantly facing awful treatment due to racism. She'd had her own fair share of it as a world-renowned basketball player.

With the popularity of her team and her talent as an individual player, her act of protest brought a lot of attention to the issue of racism. She lost many fans for this act, and for a while, she seemed to face even more issues as a Black woman because of it as well. But she stood firm in her beliefs and the need for these attitudes to change. How impressive!

It takes a lot of courage to speak out when you believe something is not right, and Maya showed a lot of bravery in this moment.

She showed even more when she decided to take a break from professional basketball in 2019. You might be wondering why, when she was at the height of one of the most successful women's basketball careers in history, Maya chose to take a break. Well, she decided to pause playing basketball so she could dedicate her time to freeing a wrongly accused man from prison.

That's right! Maya paused her amazingly successful basketball career to help someone in need. And not just anyone — it was someone she loved dearly. It was time to try her hand at winning on another kind of court.

Maya had met Jonathan Irons through her godparents when she was young. They immediately became friends, and he was like family to her. When he was just 16 years old, Jonathan was accused of stealing and hurting someone.

It was a crime he had not committed, but despite being so young and trying to convince a judge and jury, he was found guilty and sentenced to prison for 50 years. That's a really long time for someone so young...

But Maya believed in her friend. She never gave up on him, and she was determined to prove he was innocent. In 2016, Maya created the Win With Justice organization to fight for changes in the criminal justice system. She wanted to raise awareness about the unfair treatment that certain people or certain groups of people — like the Black community — experienced from judges, lawyers, and police officers.

Due to many incorrect beliefs that the African American community is more likely to commit crimes than others, they are often targeted and blamed when a crime is committed, and this is what happened with Jonathan.

She felt that this was exactly what had caused her dear friend to be accused of a crime he had not committed. She firmly believed Jonathan did not deserve to be sent to prison, because there hadn't been enough evidence during the trial to prove he had committed the crime.

Even after he had gone to prison, Maya and Jonathan had kept up their friendship by writing letters, speaking on the phone, and meeting in person. Slowly, Maya and Jonathan fell in love, making her all the more determined to prove his innocence.

In 2019, Maya decided to use her fame as a basketball player to bring in support and pushed for the case to be looked at again. She felt that Jonathan had only been sentenced because he had been the easy person to accuse because of the bias against Black people.

It was only when Maya became involved that a judge looked at the case again. When that judge decided to get involved, Maya shared with him all the proof she had gathered for Jonathan's innocence.

After spending many, many hours going over the case, Maya had found lots of moments throughout the investigation that didn't seem right to her. For example, no one under the age of 18 is allowed to be spoken to by police without a parent. Jonathan had only been 16 when he was accused, but they only ever spoke to him without his parents around. That's really unfair!

There was also no proof that Jonathan had ever been in the area or around the person he had been accused of hurting. So, it wasn't fair that he got blamed for the crimes and sent to prison.

Finally, one judge listened to Maya's reasoning, and he agreed that Jonathan was indeed innocent. In March of 2020, Jonathan was officially released from prison. He was free to live his life and to have a relationship with Maya.

They were married only nine days after his release. What a love story! They are now working together to fight against unfairness and help others overcome a system that is not always fair for everyone. Jonathan is also helping those in prison understand their legal options.

But unfortunately, this doesn't change the all wrong that had been done to Jonathan. He had to spend 20 years in prison when he should not have had to.

If it hadn't been for Maya's platform as an international basketball star, Jonathan would have never been proven innocent. It was likely no one was ever going to look at his case again, and Jonathan would have spent the rest of his life in prison. And this was what Maya was fighting against. She was determined to make sure the rules and justice system are fair and right for everyone.

No one should have to feel what Jonathan felt, so Maya works hard to help the world change the way it approaches these things. She officially announced her retirement from basketball in 2023 after a three-year break, and she now spends most of her time working with her organization, Win With Justice, to bring awareness to social issues.

Just by doing this, Maya made basketball history. Many commentators were shocked that such a successful player would decide to end their career at the height of it. But overall, they were all impressed. The fact that Maya chose to be a spokesperson for justice instead of pursuing fame and continuing to play basketball shows that she is not only a winner on the basketball court but a winner in life, too.

Since their marriage, Jonathan and Maya have written a memoir about both their lives, *Love and Justice: A Story of Triumph on Two Different Courts*. In it, Jonathan shares his experience fighting against unfairness, and Maya shares her story about her success on the basketball court. Their stories come together amazingly as their love overcame such hardships.

Taking a stand against unfairness is a tough task. It requires bravery to speak up against what's not right. But Maya saw problems within the criminal justice system and said something about them. She said, "If the hearts of the people are not about justice, then any system you have won't work."

Maya Moore is truly a champion on and off the basketball court. She reached the top of her basketball game and was not afraid to let that go to search for justice for someone who couldn't. Maya has shown the world that you should always speak up for those who cannot. She could have continued to play basketball, and Jonathan would still be in prison. Instead, she decided to give that up to help someone in need.

Maya's decision to close the chapter on her basketball journey has, in fact, opened a new and exciting door that teaches us even more important life lessons. Maya is a great team player — when she won championships, she did it with her team, and when she helped Jonathan, she made him part of her team to support him. Her story teaches us that working together and treating everyone fairly is one of the most important things we can do.

Jackie Joyner-Kersee

Jackie Joyner-Kersee jumped her way to becoming one of the most famous track-and-field athletes in the world. And I mean that literally! As one of the best long jumpers in history, Jackie gave everything she had to everything she did. And through her career, she changed not only the landscape of sports but also the whole world.

Jackie was born in East St. Louis, Illinois, on March 3, 1962. When she was born, Jackie's grandmother took one look at her granddaughter and said Jackie would be first at something, so she needed a "First Lady kind of name."

Taking her mother's advice, Jackie's mother decided to name her new daughter Jacqueline after President John F. Kennedy's wife, the First Lady of America at the time. Well, Jackie's grandmother was right! Jackie came first in many ways, proving herself to be a winner through her determination and dedication.

Jackie's parents were very young when they started their family, but they knew the value of a good education. They wanted their children to do well in school, so they pushed their kids to always do their best and take advantage of school and everything it offered.

Jackie and her brother, Al, were both good athletes, but Jackie was truly excellent at sports. She played basketball, volleyball, and track throughout her school days. Not many people can balance so many sports! Because of her talent in so many different sporting fields, she decided to try out one of the hardest types of races ever invented: the pentathlon.

This competition includes swimming, running, horseback riding, shooting, and fencing. That's a lot wrapped into one competition, but she had what it took to be successful!

Jackie didn't win just one; she won FOUR back-to-back National Junior Pentathlon championships! Not only that, but as a junior in high school, she set the girls' Illinois state record for the long jump. Whoa, that's incredible, and it's a lot to do just in high school! It was clear to everyone that Jackie was destined to be great.

Jackie's talents in basketball and track earned her a scholarship to the University of California Los Angeles (UCLA). Jackie was all set to head to university in 1980 when her mother suddenly died.

Losing her mom was hard for Jackie, but instead of letting it take over, she decided to work even harder to make her mom proud. Her mother had always wanted Jackie to be a success, so Jackie was going to make sure her mother could look down on her and smile. Jackie went to UCLA, ready to try her best after taking a little time to say goodbye to her mother.

That year, Jackie decided to start training for the heptathlon, one of the most challenging sports events in the world. Yes, it is even harder than the pentathlon! Instead of only five sporting trials, the heptathlon has *seven!*

In this competition, athletes must compete in seven different competitions over the course of two days: 100-meter hurdles, high jump, shot put, 200-meter run, long jump, javelin throw, and 800-meter run.

While Jackie had already impressed during the pentathlon, she felt she was ready to improve her game and match the new competition in the Olympics. So, with the help of her assistant track coach Bob Kersee, she began to train hard. I can't even imagine just how hard it was!

Jackie's successes in track and field were particularly outstanding. Not only did many people believe that she wouldn't do well at the sport because she was a woman, but she also had many doubters because she was Black. But Jackie was dedicated and trained hard. She decided that she would be the best she could be, despite what others thought about her skin color and gender.

Jackie's time to shine came when she competed in the Olympic heptathlon for the first time during the 1984 Summer Olympic Games in Los Angeles. But it wasn't perfect. While gearing up for the competition, Jackie pulled her hamstring, an important muscle in the leg for running, jumping, and swimming.

There was no way Jackie could recover in time for the game, but she chose to compete anyway. She was determined not to let her hard work go to waste over a small strain! So, Jackie competed, and more impressively, she won second place!

Jackie took home the silver medal that year after losing the gold by only five points. Five measly points! While it had not been the perfect competition, she was proud that she had pushed through.

Now, she was even more determined. She had been so close to winning first place, and she could taste it! She was set on getting the gold medal in the next competition. So, with the help of her coach, Bob, she got back to training.

Bob and Jackie made a great team, but not just in sports. During their training, they actually fell in love, and Jackie married Bob in 1986. Their relationship was unique because Bob continued to coach her even after they were married – what great teamwork they showed.

The following year, Jackie competed in the 1987 Goodwill Games in Moscow. Jackie won this competition by miles and set the world record for the most points earned during a heptathlon. She was officially the first person to ever score over 7,000 points for the event. If you don't know much about heptathlons, that's a whole lot of points!

But this wasn't nearly the end for Jackie. In the 1988 Olympics in Seoul, Jackie finally took home the gold medal. Then, she turned around and did the same thing in 1992! With these wins, she was the first heptathlete to win the gold medal back-to-back, on top of beating her own scoring record three more times. Talk about setting world records!

Even while setting record-breaking scores, Jackie said, "The medals don't mean anything, and the glory doesn't last. It's all about your happiness.

The rewards are going to come, but my happiness is just loving the sport and having fun performing."

It was refreshing for the world to hear such a successful athlete say this about their success. It is easy to think that winning will automatically bring happiness, but that was not what made Jackie happy. She genuinely enjoyed playing her sport and competing, and that was what fulfilled her life, not just winning. She would have enjoyed the sport whether or not she won because it was what made her happy.

Although Jackie loved competing, the strain of these events did cause some difficulties. Jackie suffered from asthma, a lung disease that can make it hard to breathe. For an athlete who has to breathe properly to do their best, this was hard to get used to. Athletes need proper airflow to keep up their energy for their sport.

Jackie refused to let this condition stop her from competing, but it was a struggle. It took a while to get the disease under control so that it wouldn't cause issues in the competition.

In athletic events, competitors are not allowed to take medicines that might make them unfairly better than their opponents. Many asthma medicines contain ingredients that can make someone more energetic or more awake, which is why they are not allowed in competitions. If one athlete is more awake than another because of medicine, there is a big chance they would do better at the competition, which is really unfair. So, it was not an option for Jackie to treat her asthma properly if she wanted to continue competing in heptathlons.

Because of her struggles with asthma, Jackie decided to create awareness of the condition among athletes. She attended a health fair at Millis Regional Health Education Center. According to their data, over 73,000 people in the area had asthma at that time. With this, she tried to prove to the sports world that asthma was a real issue that many people, not just athletes, struggled with. She felt they deserved to be treated equally since it affected so many parts of her life, not just sports.

Many parts of competing were difficult for Jackie because of her asthma. She had to travel a lot for competitions, which meant constantly changing her environment. Traveling to different climates and temperatures can cause issues for those with asthma. If you are visiting somewhere very cold one day, then somewhere very hot the next, you can imagine it does not feel very good for your lungs!

The Olympics are held all over the world, in different places each time. Jackie found it very frustrating to have to think about how to avoid an asthma attack every time she wanted to take part in a competition. She always had to make sure she had a local doctor who could help her if she had any difficulties, which took up a lot of time, money, and energy.

Another thing that can trigger asthma is just being outside. Sometimes, there is a lot of pollen, which is dust produced by plants, in the air. On these days, Jackie would have to wear a mask to avoid triggering an asthma attack. She had a lot of allergies to grass, which made it hard to be outside without triggering her breathing issues — especially at track-and-field events. They're absolutely *covered* in grass!

That makes it really difficult to avoid for some athletes. And for those who cannot take their proper medicine because the sport bans it? It was next to impossible for Jackie to compete without having an attack!

An asthma attack can be very frightening. It makes it difficult to breathe, and if an athlete is already trying to catch their breath, an asthma attack can be dangerous. On one occasion, Jackie had to go to hospital for two days to get over one. How scary! It even made the news, and an article in the *Washington Post* appeared about her struggle with asthma and allergies.

As a response, she said, "I can control so much of what I do, and I can't control this asthma. Sometimes, I don't want to accept that I have asthma."

For Jackie, it often felt like she was not in control of herself or her ability to live her life fully because of her asthma.

"All I ever wanted, really, and continue to want out of life, is to give 100 percent to whatever I'm doing and then let the results speak for themselves," she said. It was difficult to balance the struggle with asthma and her desire to give everything she had.

What Jackie taught the world in her moments of struggle is that even on bad days, if you decide to give it all you have that day, then you did your best. And if that was enough for Jackie, then that is enough for the rest of us.

For her, her success was all about consistency. Her career was built on always showing up. If she consistently showed up for training and listened to her coaches, then she was happy with the small improvements she made each day. Even a tiny bit of progress was important progress. It meant she was going in the right direction: forward.

If she could take 10 seconds off her running time or add half an inch to her jump, then she felt that was progress and meant she was doing something right. To her, it was small steps that led to improvement and strengthened her, meaning she could do her best.

Jackie was an amazing and inspirational athlete throughout her career. If she could have competed for her whole life, she would have. But another hamstring injury during the 1996 Olympics forced her to retire. Jackie did not want to give up, but her husband (and coach) reminded her that she risked hurting herself more if she did not stop.

There were lots of tears, but Jackie agreed not to compete in the heptathlon for her health. Still determined to do what she loved, she stayed for the long jump competition and took home the bronze medal. While this decision was difficult for Jackie, it was the right one. Sometimes, making the right decision is hard. But Jackie needed to take care of herself, so that's what she did.

A few years later, Jackie retired from sports and moved into charity work and motivational speaking. In 1988, she started the Jackie Joyner-Kersee Foundation to help at-risk children. After retiring, she threw all of her attention into this work.

In addition to this foundation, she partnered with several other athletes to form Athletes for Hope. This organization helps connect professional athletes to ways they can help their communities. And later, Jackie worked with Comcast to get laptops and Internet services for low-income families. Since it was created, the program has given Internet access to nearly six million families!

Jackie really cares about making things fair for everyone. She wrote two books: *A Kind of Grace* and *A Woman's Place is Everywhere*. One book is about her life growing up to be one of the world's greatest female athletes, and the other shares stories of inspiring women, showing that everyone can do great things.

She talks a lot about ensuring people are treated equally, regardless of their race or whether they're a boy or a girl, and ensuring kids have a good education and can stay healthy.

Even after a successful career as an athlete, Jackie carried on her efforts to have a positive impact on the world after her retirement. She used her stage to share important lessons about staying healthy, helping families who need it, and speaking up for girls' right to a fair and equal life.

Kids just like you can take inspiration from Jackie's attitude. "It is better to look ahead and prepare, than to look back and regret," she said. She took what she learned through sports — the importance of training hard — and used it in her everyday life. She learned that preparing ahead of time and working hard pays off.

Preparation leads to success. If you have a test, prepare by studying. If you have a sports match coming up, prepare by going to practice. Whatever you are doing in life — prepare. It takes mental and physical strength to be prepared, but if you do, you will always be able to look forward to success.

Megan Rapinoe

Standing out in a crowd is not everyone's idea of fun, but Megan Rapinoe is someone who speaks out, stands up, and lives by brave moments. She is someone who likes to be noticed for good reasons. To Megan, putting yourself out there and standing up for what you believe in is empowering.

Megan Rapinoe is not only a world-class soccer player but also fearless in expressing her thoughts. Megan shows us that actions truly are stronger than words, and she has a passion for making changes in the world around her.

Megan was born on July 5, 1985, in Redding, California. She has a twin sister named Rachael, and their parents, Jim and Denise, raised six children together. A big family! Megan and her sister grew up watching their older brother play soccer from a young age, and when they were around five years old themselves, they decided to give it a shot. And they shot their balls right into their goals!

They were both naturally talented players, so their parents had them join a local team to continue playing. But in their small town, there were no girls' teams, so the sisters had to play with a team of boys instead. Not having any other girls on their teams was tough, but they stood out as two of the best players. You could say that Megan was already making her mark on the world!

For most of her childhood, Megan played on teams coached by her father. But when she entered high school, Megan joined the Elk Grove Pride Club in Sacramento, California, rather than join her high school's teams. Although this other team meant her parents would have to drive over two hours for practices and games, they supported Megan's dreams.

While playing for this team, Megan was able to get the attention of many local teams and had many opportunities to play for state-level teams. Megan hoped to earn an athletic scholarship to attend college for her soccer skills. And that's when the University of Portland came into play!

Being a Portland Pilot was a great success for Megan. Both her skills and her sister's helped the Pilots go undefeated in their 2005 season. On the field, Megan had amazing timing and a gift for knowing when to take risks and when to keep the ball. She had several incredible achievements just in her first year alone.

She was invited to join the Soccer America First Team Freshmen All-America team. Then, she made the Woman's Soccer Championship All-Tournament Team and was chosen as the West Coast Freshman of the Year.

Time and time again, Megan proved herself as a very valuable player. And not just because she is super talented. Soccer is a team sport, and Megan always remembered how important it was to count on her teammates to win a game. She loved helping her teammates and getting support from them, too!

But then, in the middle of her sophomore year, Megan tore her ACL, which is the part of your body that holds your knee together. Yikes! What's worse is that she was one of the US's top scorers when it happened!

Megan was at the top of her game, but she was forced to end her season and take time off to recover. After taking the rest of the season to get better, Megan took a chance by returning to the game the following season. It was a little too soon to try her knee. Most players take a little extra time off with this kind of injury just to make sure it's fully healed and strong before they play on it again.

Megan knew it was a risk, but she wanted to try. Unfortunately, her knee was not ready to play again just yet. Her ACL was re-injured, and Megan had to leave her team for the season once more. What a frustrating time!

But while the injury was hard to cope with at the time, Megan looks back on the recovery period positively. She has said it gave her a lot of time to truly appreciate all she had achieved at such a young age. And when she officially got back to soccer, she felt stronger. She said, "The injury grounded me in a lot of different ways. The rehab process makes you stronger on all fronts, mentally and physically. I feel stronger and a better person for it."

It is rare for someone to have such a positive attitude about something so life-changing. But Megan had her head in the right place and fought her way through the challenge. Instead of worrying about the setback, Megan instead looked at the injury as a time to get even stronger. There's no better way to face disappointments.

Over her soccer career, Megan has played for several women's teams. She's played for the Chicago Red Stars, the Philadelphia Independence, Boca Raton magicJack, the Seattle Sounders Women, and more. And that was just in the US!

Megan also had a significant soccer career in several other countries. She has consistently proven herself to be a valuable player. She earned a place on the women's national team, on which she helped Team USA win the gold medal during the 2012 Summer Olympics in London.

Also during these Olympics, she became one of the few athletes ever to score an "Olimpico" goal, a goal that is scored directly from a corner kick and is next to impossible to make. She also played for the women's national team when they took home the World Cup in 2015, and in 2019, she joined them once more — but this time, as a co-captain.

That 2019 Women's World Cup was one for the history books. Megan brought her team to victory as their captain and won the Golden Boot for scoring the most goals and the Golden Ball award for being the top player. Because of all those wins, Megan was also named FIFA's Woman's World Player of the Year in 2019.

But what also made this particular game so historical was that during the final World Cup game, a video about Megan caused some trouble. You see, another reason to admire Megan is because she has always been unafraid to speak her mind and be her true self. In 2019, she was very vocal about how she did not support the U.S. president at the time, Donald Trump.

President Trump had invited Megan's USA Team to the White House after the World Cup if they won to celebrate the national accomplishment. However, Megan stood firm in her beliefs and publicly said in a video on the Internet that she would not be going to visit the president. This caused a lot of negative opinions and hateful comments to come towards Megan, but no matter what, she was strong in her beliefs — which is always something to admire.

So, the 2019 World Cup was an interesting one for Megan as she was facing online bullying while trying to be a good captain for her team. She led them to an international victory and was celebrated for her sportsmanship at the same time. I'm sure that was a weird position to be in!

But Megan handled it with grace. She was thankful for the recognition and win and did not stoop down to the online bullies' levels. Instead, she just used the moment to remind the world that she was allowed to have her own opinions and that she was going to stand up for what she believed in. This was not the first time that Megan had done just that.

Just before the London Olympics in 2012, Megan announced to the world that she was gay. This announcement caught the attention of many, but especially the LGBTQ community around the world.

The LGBTQ community is a group of people who have different ways of falling in love. Some people might like someone of the opposite gender, some of the same gender, and some don't feel strongly about either. The LGBTQ community says that everyone deserves to be treated with kindness and respect, no matter who they are or who they love.

Unfortunately, not everyone was accepting of Megan, and some were very unkind to people who were gay, especially if they were famous. Being a gay person in the spotlight can be very difficult because it can make you an easy target for hateful people.

Megan said that she was proud to be a lesbian; she became a pillar of light to those who were scared to be themselves in the same way. It sent out the message to the world that it's okay to be who you are.

Megan and her partner, Sue Bird, met at the 2016 Summer Olympics. During their very public relationship, they have done some amazing things together. They even hosted the 2020 Excellence in Sports Performance Yearly (ESPY) awards together.

They also got engaged in 2020! Because of Megan's success as a soccer player, they feel it is important to lead by example, so they have never been afraid of being together as a couple in public. To make other people feel happy like them, they founded a creative production company, A Touch More, to share stories about who they are and the communities that need attention and help.

Even when some people said unkind things about who Megan loves or her relationship, she stayed strong and didn't let it bother her. It wasn't easy to do this, of course, but she decided to be brave. It was more important to her to be true to herself. She did not want to hide who she was just because of other people's opinions, and she knew others like her were looking up to her, so she spoke her truth for them just as much as herself.

Since then, she has used her platform to speak on many important issues. She isn't afraid to share her thoughts on times when people are excluded because of their skin color or gender or when others are bullied for their beliefs. Megan constantly fights for equality — she is a woman for all! She knows people listen to her because of her success as a professional soccer player, so she uses it to make the world better.

"This is my charge to everybody. Do what you can, do what you have to do. Step outside of yourself. Be more. Be better. Be bigger than you've ever been before," she said.

And that is exactly how she leads us. She even chose to kneel during the "National Anthem" to support protests against unfair treatment based on skin color. Standing out in a crowd takes great courage when others are doing the opposite of you. But for Megan, standing up for her beliefs was worth the uncomfortable moments if it made the world a kinder place.

One of her greatest achievements was winning a legal battle against the US Soccer Federation. Megan and her fellow soccer players fought for the same pay and medical treatment as male soccer players in the federation.

When they won, Megan said, "For us, this is a huge win in ensuring that we not only right the wrongs of the past, but set the next generation up for something we only dreamed of." Because of Megan's passion and drive to help others, she made a real difference in the way this federation treated women.

Megan is known as a soccer player who has made a great mark in the history of women's soccer. And she is this and much more. She decided to retire at the end of the 2023 season and thanked her family, teammates, and coaches for their help during her career. After retirement, Megan has become more involved in helping with social issues, like the need for more leaders who are female, gay, and people of color. She also started her clothing line, Re—inc, which includes clothing to fit all gender types and all body shapes and sizes.

She has also written a book, *One Life*, about her life working to speak on different issues around the world. She did not write it so people would know her as a soccer player. She wrote it to encourage others to speak out on social issues and make a difference in the world.

Megan is not afraid to stand up for what she believes in, which is something we can all take note of. We can make a difference in the world by just speaking up when we are needed. If a friend is being bullied at school, you can help them by saying something.

Megan defends her opinions with actions that speak louder than words. She is a strong example of an athlete who shows determination and conviction about her beliefs. We should never back down from our beliefs or be afraid to be who we truly are. As Megan said, "I was made exactly the way I was meant to be made in who I am and my personality and the way I was born."

Tatyana McFadden

Would you believe that the fastest woman in the world has spent her life in a wheelchair? When Tatyana was born in a small Russian town on April 21, 1989, her life was destined to be different. She was born with a small hole in her spine, a condition known as spina bifida. Because of this, Tatyana was completely paralyzed from the waist down, and she would never be able to use her legs like others.

Shortly after she was born, Tatyana was given to a small orphanage in Russia to await adoption. Most people who are born with spina bifida are wheelchair-bound for life, and many are lucky if they can afford the wheelchairs they need.

But although her orphanage did their best to care for Tatyana's needs, they could not afford expensive equipment like a wheelchair, so Tatyana spent many years without one. This made it so hard for Tatyana to get around and play with her friends. Can you imagine just sitting while your friends run around you while having fun? That would be hard for anyone!

Well, it's a good thing that Tatyana wasn't just anyone! She didn't let this little problem stop her from living her best life. She decided that if she couldn't walk with her legs, she would just walk with her hands! Day after day, Tatyana taught herself to use her arms and legs to pull and walk herself around the orphanage. By the time she was six years old, she was zooming around with the rest of her friends.

Tatyana was born special in more ways than one. Not only was she different because of her medical condition, but she was also born with courage. Instead of letting her circumstances bring her down, Tatyana learned to walk on her hands so that she could play like a normal girl. It wasn't perfect, but Tatyana refused to miss the best parts of life just because her legs worked differently than everyone else's.

For the first six years of her life, Tatyana decided to embrace her disability every day as she waited for the day someone might choose to adopt her.

Lucky for her, when she was six years old, Deborah McFadden was visiting Russia on a business trip. As the Commissioner of Disabilities for the US Department of Health, Deborah traveled a lot for work. But she never expected this trip to bring her a daughter.

During a fateful visit to Tatyana's orphanage, Deborah immediately connected to the little girl. And before her trip was over, Tatyana was adopted and set to go back home to the US with her new mother.

After Tatyana was settled into her new family, her parents encouraged Tatyana to try sports to strengthen her muscles. But after years of walking on her hands, Tatyana already had a pretty powerful upper body and arms. So, she found a home in the sport of wheelchair racing, where her strong arms could push her to victory.

Tatyana officially began wheelchair racing at eight years old. If you are not familiar with wheelchair racing, it is a track-and-field event for disabled individuals without the use of their legs. It is one of the most popular events at the Paralympics, the Olympic competition specifically for those with disabilities.

There are very strict rules attached to wheelchair racing. Para-athletes are put into different categories based on their disabilities. It's a bit like weight classes in able-bodied sports.

Tatyana is classified as a T54, meaning she is fully functional from the waist up and specifically competes in track events in a wheelchair. But racing wheelchairs are different than normal, everyday wheelchairs. They have two large wheels at the back and one small wheel at the front to improve the wheelchair's speed and performance. Everything on a racing wheelchair is designed to make it faster, more comfortable, and easier to manage than a regular chair.

As Tatyana's love for wheelchair racing grew, so did her talent. Her mother worked hard to help Tatyana's schools and communities understand how to properly provide what she and others like her needed.

Many were happy to include Tatyana and liked having her join in because it taught them about the importance of inclusion. After all, Tatyana was just another little girl, even though she was in a wheelchair.

Unfortunately, Tatyana's high school experience was not so welcoming. After competing in small meets for wheelchair racing since she was eight, Tatyana tried to join her high school track team.

Instead of welcoming her, they told her that her wheelchair took up too much space, so she would not be able to race at the same time as the able-bodied runners. While this disappointed Tatyana, their rejection only lit her fire.

Her high school dismissed her because she was in a wheelchair. This is called discrimination. It meant her high school was disobeying the Americans with Disabilities Act (ADA). In 1990, this act was passed to protect those with disabilities from discrimination just like this.

Instead of just letting the school do this, she decided to sue the school system for excluding her from the race. But it wasn't for money. She just wanted the right to join in with high school sports like any other student.

Tatyana won her legal battle, and was given the right to race. Because of her bravery, the state of Maryland now requires all schools to give students with disabilities the chance to take part in all sports. Eventually, Tatyana pressed for the same kind of law to be applied across the entire US. Now, that law is a reality. Go, Tatyana!

For Tatyana, life was not easy in the beginning, but she kept going through everything that stood in her way. Her determination not only won her the chance to continue doing what she loved but also conquered the entire sport.

In 2004, she took part in her first Paralympics in Athens. At just 15 years old, she was the youngest member of the team, but that didn't stop her from winning both a silver and a bronze medal. She impressed many people, but this win just gave Tatyana a taste for more. From then on, she was determined to get better and become the best she could be.

And that's exactly what she did! For four years, she worked and trained hard. Then, in 2008, Tatyana competed in the Beijing Paralympics and earned four more medals — three silver and one bronze. She'd worked hard, and that hard work paid off once again!

But at this point, Tatyana loved the competition and was striving to get better and better. So, in 2009, she decided to branch out from her short wheelchair races and try her skills in a marathon. She wanted to use this as a way to train for longer distance runs in her competitions.

That year, she won first place in the women's wheelchair division at the Chicago Marathon, finishing in just one hour, 50 minutes, and 47 seconds. That's pretty impressive!

In 2012, her training and determination paid off even more. Tatyana returned to the Paralympics in London and won three gold medals! This was just the beginning of Tatyana's winning streak. The very next year, Tatyana took home six gold medals at the World Championships and became the first athlete in history to win six gold medals at the same competition.

Then, she set another record by becoming the first person to win four Major Marathons in the same year, also known as the Grand Slam. Plus, she did the same thing three more times! Could she get any more impressive?

After winning a silver medal at the Paralympics in 2014, Tatyana competed again in 2016 in Rio. And here, she not only won but also set the record for the most medals won by a US track-and-field athlete at a Paralympics since 1992.

Tatyana's achievements are very impressive. She is a 20-time Paralympic medalist, a 20-time World Championship medalist, and a 24-time winner at the Abbott World Marathon Majors, an international competition of the world's hardest marathons. This achievement gave her more marathon wins than any other female wheelchair athlete.

It is impressive that anyone could achieve so much, but it is especially impressive that Tatyana did it with a disability. She shows us that if you work hard and prepare, you can do more than you ever thought you could. The obstacles in our paths shape us and help us become stronger. Difficulties will always be part of life, and that will never change. What we can change is how we let them affect us.

Tatyana's obstacle was her disability, but she's never seen it as something negative. Many call her brave because of this mindset, but to this, Tatyana replies, "For me, 'my brave' was an act of acceptance. Accepting myself as I am."

Acceptance is a powerful life lesson. There are some things in life we can change and some things we must accept. Tatyana accepted she would never be able to walk, but she did not sit back and do nothing. She pushed through her difficulties and became a Paralympic champion despite all the challenges. To her, "Life isn't about what you don't have. It's what you do with the gifts you have been given."

Part of accepting herself meant accepting that she was just as worthy as any other runner, even though her racing world was a little different. Tatyana does not think of herself as someone with a disability. She just thinks of herself as a runner, and she works hard to achieve and do what she loves.

She trains just as hard, if not harder, as runners who don't have a disability. She even earned the nickname "The Beast" because of how hard she trained, doing things like climbing stairs on her hands to keep her arms and hands strong.

The challenges of being a Paralympic athlete are both physical and mental. Tatyana regularly works with a psychologist to keep her mental health in good shape. Since she began doing this, she has expressed just how much calmer her thoughts are. Things like meditation and journaling are fantastic for those who face stressful situations, like athletes.

Tatyana still strives to win every race she enters, but it is no longer about just winning. It's about doing what she loves and working hard for her goal. Before a race, she tries to visualize exactly how she will win the race by creating a picture in her mind.

This helps Tatyana feel like her goals are not out of reach. If she can see herself doing it, then she can do it. This is true of any goal, too. If you ever doubt that you are capable of achieving your goal, just think of yourself actually reaching the goal. Picture how you are going to face the challenge in your mind, then use that to work out the steps you plan to take to succeed.

Tatyana has mentioned just how many great life lessons she has learned from racing and doing marathons. A big one she learned was to celebrate each victory, no matter whether it was big or small. Every little success is important. They each prove just how hard you worked, which means they each deserve to be celebrated.

And there are opportunities to celebrate small successes every day. Try to notice the little things that add up to the bigger things in your life and let yourself feel proud of those things. Feel pleased when you do better than you expected in the classroom or at home.

It is easy to focus on the losses, but celebrating every small victory will strengthen your belief in yourself. When you believe in yourself, there is nothing that can stop you from winning and reaching that goal.

In 2020, Tatyana became the first person with a disability to be put into the Hall of Fame for her achievements in distance running. What a win!

Since then, she has been helping support charitable work for disabled children. She recently helped create a playground for children of all abilities to be able to play together. She sees inclusion as an important part of children's lives. So, she works to make sure all children can enjoy life, regardless of their physical abilities.

Tatyana wrote a book to focus on spreading awareness of disabled athletes and their capabilities. She titled the book *Ya Sama! Moments from My Life*. In Russian, "Ya Sama" means "I can do it."

Her purpose behind the book was to inspire everyone and say that you can triumph over adversity, even when it seems like life is not on your side. She has done the same thing by producing *Rising Phoenix*, a documentary about her and other disabled athletes' experiences.

Her entire career has been dedicated to proving false beliefs about those with disabilities wrong. She said, "For me, I am proud to be disabled and an athlete. I think the more we talk about it and provide education, the more inclusive world we can be."

Inclusion is now a big part of everything Tatyana does. She uses every opportunity to showcase the importance of including those with disabilities. She proves everyone in life is equally valuable, whether they are disabled or not.

She has said that acknowledging someone's disability is not a bad or offensive thing. It is a part of who they are, and it is a good thing to talk about it. The more we make this feel normal, the more others will realize that being disabled doesn't mean someone can't take care of themselves or do things well.

Tatyana has taught us that everyone deserves equal respect, no matter what their condition is. Just because someone is different does not mean they are less worthy of respect.

Tatyana is not just someone with a disability. She is a 17-time Paralympic medalist, 23-time marathon winner, and the fastest woman in the world. And she just happened to be born with spina bifida. She has shown the entire world how courage and determination can overcome all obstacles. Just like in her documentary, *Rising Phoenix,* she proves that when it feels like the world has burned us, we can indeed rise from the ashes.

Bethany Hamilton

Bethany Hamilton was born to surf.

Bethany was born on February 8, 1990, as the youngest member of a surfing family. From the very beginning, surfing was in her DNA! The whole Hamilton family loved surfing, including her two brothers, her mom, and her dad.

Unsurprisingly, she was out in the waves on her surfboard, learning to surf by the time she was three years old. Growing up in Lihue, a small town on the Hawaiian island of Kauai, meant her love of surfing had plenty of room to grow.

Island life was a beautiful fairy tale for a young Bethany. Up until the sixth grade, Bethany joined many other island kids in their local school. It was completely normal to show up to school with sandy feet and wet hair after a morning ride on the waves!

From sixth grade on, she was homeschooled by her mom, which meant that Bethany was able to spend all of her free time surfing. Like many other families on her island, a typical day for Bethany was waking up early and starting her day surfing. Then, when it was time for schooling, she went back home to complete her studies. And when school was finished for the day, she was back out on the water, surfing again.

When Bethany was eight years old, she started to take part in surfing competitions, and she was so good that she got her first sponsorship by the time she was nine years old. Surfing was not cheap, and gaining a sponsor meant Bethany could get gear in exchange for promoting the company that provided it.

Even though Bethany was young, she was starting to make a career for herself out of sheer passion and dedication. In 2003, at only 13 years old, she won second place in the women's division of the National Scholastic Surfing Association (NSSA) National Championships. Bethany was on the fast track for a superstar surfing career!

Then, the worst happened. Just a few months after her win, every surfer's fear came true for Bethany. The ocean is a large space where many unique creatures live. The ocean is nothing to fear, but it is something to respect. Every surfer knows this, but there is one creature that all surfers avoid because of their sheer power: sharks.

On October 31, 2003, Bethany was out surfing with a friend at Tunnels Beach, a well-known beach in Hawaii. After riding the waves, Bethany took a break and relaxed in the water. As she lay on her surfboard, enjoying the sun, with her left arm lazily dangling in the water, she was unaware of what was to come.

The next thing she knew, a large mouth had hold of her left arm, and she was being roughly yanked back and forth in the water.

Bethany had been attacked by a shark. A 14-foot tiger shark, to be exact. Mistaking Bethany for an animal, the shark attacked, and by the time it realized its mistake, Bethany's arm was already gone.

Bethany clung to her board as the shark swam away and her friend called for help. As Bethany was rushed to hospital, she lost more than half the blood in her body. Most humans cannot survive such an injury, but Bethany fought. After several surgeries, Bethany awoke to a different world – one where she had no left arm and little possibility that she would ever surf again.

Bethany's life was completely changed. Her entire world looked different now that she had no left arm to use. Think of all the things you do in a day with your hands. Now, think of only using one. It's quite a difference! And for Bethany, it greatly affected the biggest part of her life: surfing.

Surfers require a lot of balance and control to do what they do. It's a lot like skating. If you aren't balanced, you're going to fall over! Losing her left arm meant Bethany's balance was completely different. Try balancing on one leg without using one of your arms. It's hard! Bethany would have to completely relearn how to balance herself if she wanted to surf. And this felt nearly impossible right after the attack.

It was a very hard time, but Bethany Hamilton was not going to give up. Surfing had been her life until this happened, and she wasn't going to let this accident change her. She trusted that this had happened for a reason, and the world was her oyster. She could either let her sadness pull her down, or she could try to look at this as an opportunity. She had great courage and determination – so guess which option she chose?

It was shocking how soon Bethany wanted to be back on her surfboard. Many expected her to be terrified of the water and the creatures inside it. I know I would have been super scared! Bethany was braver than most people, though. Instead of letting herself be afraid of sharks or be scared of having to learn how to surf all over again, Bethany decided to choose determination, hard work, and bravery.

For the month following her injury, Bethany worked hard to learn how to shift her weight and control her surfing without her arm. It took a lot of work. At first, she fell off her board a lot more than she stayed on. It involved a lot of heartache and a lot of failing.

The important part, though? Bethany always got back up and tried again. She knew that if she kept working hard, she would eventually be just as good as she was before! A month later, Bethany was back out on the water with no left arm but a whole lot of bravery and determination.

"It's not about how many times you get knocked down that counts, it's about how many times you get back up!" said Bethany. This was the motto that Bethany focused on as she relearned how to surf. She focused on the idea that nothing is impossible if you try hard and get back up every time you fail. What a motto!

Failure does not mean we have lost. Failures just mean that we have more to learn. Each time Bethany fell off her board, she chose to learn from that failure by figuring out her mistake, learning from it, and trying again. She was brave enough to hold on to this, and remember, she was only 13 years old! After deciding that she could surf again with one arm, Bethany set her mind to it and worked until she achieved her goal.

In 2004, Bethany participated in her first competition with one arm. It was such an inspiring event, it earned national attention. And Bethany's hard work paid off. Only a few months after her attack, she placed fifth in a regional competition. Fifth! With one arm! Only a few months after she had lost her entire left arm. Talk about being an inspiration! She not only beat the odds of surfing again, but she proved those who doubted her wrong.

Instead of letting fear conquer her, Bethany decided that she could overcome it. She didn't want to be held back by what had happened to her, so she let her love of surfing heal her instead.

But she was honest about what getting back out on her board meant. Many called her "brave" and "courageous" for doing so, and she was. But to her, being courageous didn't mean that she wasn't afraid. "Courage means you don't let fear stop you," she said.

Bethany was honest that she had many moments when she was afraid. She was afraid of the water and afraid of failing, but she continued to get up, try again, and work hard. And by 2005, Bethan had earned a national championship title by winning first place in the NSSA National Championship.

Since then, Bethany has found her way into international surfing competitions, written books, appeared in movies, gotten married, and started a family. She not only relearned how to surf, but she improved and got even better than she was before losing her arm. Now, she is one of the leading female surfers in the entire world!

She has competed in the World Surf League (WSL), toured the entire world, and won countless awards for her skills. She has won awards around the world, from America to Australia, and even Portugal and Peru.

Bethany is now known as a "pipeline champion" and came first in the T & C Pipeline Woman's Pro in 2007. A pipeline wave is a very high wave that curls over at the top and makes a tunnel. When surfers take on a pipeline wave, they aim to surf through the whole length of the tunnel and come out on the other end with no problem. It is one of the most difficult and dangerous kinds of waves to surf. But Bethany? She *conquered* them!

While Bethany is an impressive athlete, she is also dedicated to using her story to inspire others. She wants others to know that facing your fears isn't impossible and that it is an important step in healing. She even donated her surfboard from her accident to the California Surf Museum to serve as a reminder of this. It still sits there, with a large bite taken out of it from that fateful day.

Another part of what Bethany says has made her successful is her faith. She was raised as a Christian and has continued to practice this as her religion throughout her life. Her faith in God's plan for her is a large part of what helped her heal after her attack. Now, she uses her voice to spread trust in God and Christian beliefs through her story. She feels that if it helped her, it might help others like her.

As you can see, her life is not just about surfing. Bethany is a symbol of hope that anyone can overcome whatever they set their mind to. Bethany used her inspirational story and became a mentor for faith and healing. The message she gives is one of hope, determination, and faith. She wants others to realize they can get back up, even if they feel like they cannot.

Bethany also supports several charities and has one of her own called the Beautifully Flawed Foundation. Through the foundation, Bethany organizes youth events and retreats for young people who have lost limbs. They are given exercises to improve balance, physical awareness, strength, stress management, and self-worth. These retreats are meant to provide survivors with a community to lean on as they heal.

Alongside this, Bethany hosts conferences for girls and young women every year, like Anchored in Love. This is to help the participants discover their true beauty and self-worth. Bethany and her husband, Adam Dirks, also run a men's retreat, Forge, to encourage young men to build faith and fitness.

During her recovery, Bethany found huge comfort in physical exercise. She had to do it to get her body strong again after her attack, but since then, it has helped her feel good about herself. Many might not expect a woman with one arm to be so active, but boy does she prove them wrong!

Bethany has never been disappointed by the loss of her arm. She says, "I wouldn't change what happened to me because then I wouldn't have this chance… to embrace more people than I ever could have with two arms." Without her experience, she would have never been able to reach others in the same ways she has.

Since her shark attack in 2003, Bethany has written several books. The first book she wrote was *Soul Surfer*, a book about her life and how she lost her arm in a shark attack, but not her faith and her spirit.

Since then, she has written several other books, including the children's book *Surfing Past Fear*. In it, Bethany uses the example of a little girl breaking her arm to showcase how children can overcome their fears. What a great message!

Now, Bethany is a wife and a mom to three boys and a girl and a world-renowned surfer, motivational speaker, and author. In everything she does, Bethany remembers what losing her arm taught her: faith, resilience, and determination.

Despite losing her arm, Bethany still plays tennis, goes hiking, and just enjoys living her life. "Life is a lot like surfing," she says. "When you get caught in the impact zone, you've got to get back up. Because you never know what may be over the next wave."

Wilma Rudolph

On June 23, 1940, in Saint Bethlehem, Tennessee, one of the most important women in the history of sports was born. The woman who became the first American woman to win three gold medals in a single Olympics. The woman who paved the way for all women of color to be able to chase their dreams. Who was this woman, you may ask? This woman was Wilma Rudolph.

When Wilma was born, she was very small because she had been born a little too early. She only weighed four-and-a-half pounds at birth. She was also from a very large family. Her father had 22 children in total, and she was the lucky number 20! So many siblings to play with!

After Wilma was born, the family moved to Clarksville, Tennessee for better work. At the time, Wilma's parents were very humble people. Wilma's dad was a railway porter, and her mom was a domestic worker. Because of her small-town beginnings, no one ever expected her to turn out to be one of the fastest women in the world!

Wilma did not have an easy start in life. Her early birth had not only left her small, but it also left her a little weak. Over and over again, Wilma got sick with different illnesses. It was like she never got better! After battling scarlet fever, double pneumonia, and polio, Wilma was left weak and unable to walk because of issues with her left leg.

She could barely walk on her own, so Wilma's mother had to take her to the hospital 50 miles away in Nashville for treatment every week. Sadly, the doctors were not very hopeful that Wilma would ever be able to walk with how bad her leg was. She was given a leg brace and a special shoe to help her learn to walk, but many doubted it would work.

But they didn't know who they were talking about yet! Despite the doctors' doubts, Wilma's mother told her daughter she *would* walk again! Wilma decided to believe her mother rather than that doubtful doctor.

With this determination and support from her mother, Wilma did indeed get better. Wilma's mother kept taking Wilma to physical therapy to work on her leg, and when Wilma was at home, her family would massage her leg four times a day just to help it improve. Wouldn't that be nice? She wore her leg brace and a special shoe for about two years, and by the time she was 11, she could walk without the brace or the shoe.

After a difficult childhood of being unable to walk, Wilma was finally on her way to feeling strong. She was homeschooled at first, but then Wilma decided to start formal school when she was seven.

In high school, she attended the all-Black Burt High School. During this time, America was segregated, which meant Black Americans could not go to the same schools as White people.

In fact, many things in the world were separated for people with different skin colors. Black people were told to use separate restrooms, water fountains, coffee machines, and more. This was a time when Black people were treated unfairly because of their skin color. It was not uncommon for Black people to be bullied or hurt just for having non-white skin. But Wilma was not going to let others' unfair beliefs stop her!

Right after Wilma mastered walking, she found herself drawn to sports. Her mother was shocked to find her outside playing with a basketball when she was just 11 years old. She was a natural athlete! Imagine going from not being able to walk to becoming a skilled sportswoman. In high school, Wilma joined the basketball team, and her talent took her all the way to being nominated as one of her state's best players.

Her grace and speed on the basketball court were so good they actually caught the attention of a track-and-field coach at Tennessee State University. That coach approached Wilma and told her she should consider running for her high school's track team. So, that's exactly what she did. And she loved it!

Running was where she shone the brightest. Her coach gave her the nickname "Skeeter," a slang word for a mosquito, because she was little, fast, and always got in the way. Sounds just like a mosquito, right? When she was asked how she had gotten so fast, she said, "I don't know why I run so fast. I just run."

And run she did! With this show of faith in her skills, Wilma became determined to prove to herself that her skills were as great as they said. "I ran and ran and ran every day, and I acquired this sense of determination, this sense of spirit that I would never give up, no matter what else happened," she said.

Wilma was so naturally talented that they let her compete with college athletes, even though she was still in high school. That must have been so cool! When she was 16 years old, she qualified for her first Olympics. While this was something that had happened before, it was still a huge deal to be considered for the Olympics while still so young!

Not only was this impressive because she was so young, but it was not easy for African American women to make a name for themselves at this time. The Civil Rights Movement surrounded Wilma's world during the first two decades of her life. African American communities were protesting against abuse and demanding to be treated equally. It wasn't fair or equal to treat people differently just because of their skin color.

Before this movement began, most sports events were filled with only White athletes. Even after it began, many White Americans wanted to use the violence during protests as an excuse to leave out Black people. Wilma was growing up and joining sports at this time in history when Black women were struggling for basic human rights. This made her spot in the 1956 Olympics even more meaningful.

That year, she won a bronze medal in the 4 x 100 relay race. This was a huge accomplishment for Wilma. Her family didn't even have plumbing in their house at the time! No one expected a little girl from Saint Bethlehem who had been unable to walk just a few years earlier to win a bronze medal for running!

It was incredible, but it only gave Wilma a small taste of what she really wanted. She wanted to win a gold medal next! After returning home from her win, she felt even more determined to continue training and getting better. She'd fallen in love with running, and it was all she wanted to do.

When she was 17 years old, she became pregnant and had to take a break from track to care for herself and her growing baby. At first, she was worried that having a baby so young would mean the end of her running career.

However, her very caring family decided to look after the baby once she was born for Wilma so she could go to college and continue training. It was such a big deal for her to have such support from her family. So, only a few months after having her child, Wilma left her baby in the good care of her family and set off for Tennessee State University.

Ed Temple became her coach at Tennessee State University, and while he was very passionate, he was also very strict. Ed made anyone who was late for practice run an extra lap on the field. Once, when Wilma was 30 minutes late for practice, she had to run an extra 30 laps! That sounds awful!

Finally, in 1960, Wilma had another chance to participate in the Summer Olympics in Rome, and she went to these games with one goal: to win a gold medal.

Well, she won three! Along with these three gold medals, she broke three world records. She became the first American woman to win three gold medals at a single Olympics, and her wins earned her the title of "Fastest Woman in the World."

Not only did she beat the 100- and 200-meter run records, but Wilma was also part of the team that set the world record in the 400-meter relay at 44.4 seconds. That's so fast!

She was one of the most popular athletes at that year's Olympics. It was a shock to the world that a young, Black woman had done so well. In basically 11 seconds, Wilma showed the world exactly what a young, Black woman could do! Because of her achievements, she was honored on television, and the *Associated Press* voted her as Female Athlete of the Year. Talk about making history!

The press labeled Wilma as the "Black Pearl" and the "Black Gazelle." But her experiences growing up had taught her a lot. Wilma saw an opportunity to change the world and make way for the Black athletes who would follow her.

When Wilma returned to the US for her homecoming parade, she refused to take part unless it would include both White and Black folk alike. She wanted her homecoming to be celebrated by all folks together because her win was for all of them. It was a very big deal that Wilma was so outspoken about this issue because it made a difference in the way Black folk and athletes were viewed by the world.

Many Black Americans around her at the time did not have the opportunities to speak out in the same ways. She recognized that the attention she was receiving meant that she had an opportunity to speak and have people actually listen to what she said. She felt it was important for her to do this for those who could not do the same.

She was also given the Sullivan Award as the nation's top amateur athlete in 1961. But that same year, Wilma retired from competing and followed her calling to be an educator. She then dedicated the rest of her life to teaching and coaching young athletes like herself and taking care of her family.

For a while, she focused her attention on creating girls' track teams in Chicago, since there were few to be found around the area. It was clear that athletics had a strong impact on Wilma, and she was determined to continue that impact by creating opportunities for others.

In 1974, she was named in the National Track & Field Hall of Fame, and then the International Sports Hall of Fame a few years later. She was also honored as part of the first group of names in the US Olympic Hall of Fame in 1983. That same year, she created the Wilma Rudolph Foundation to support young athletes.

Wilma is now honored every year by the Women's Sports Foundation with the Wilma Rudolph Courage Award. This award is given to a female athlete who showcases courage in the face of challenges and adversity. The first athlete to win this award was Jackie Joyner-Kersee. How cool!

Wilma constantly showed the world perseverance and dedication to her goals. Not only did she overcome the chances of never walking again as a child, but she went on to become the fastest woman in the world at the time, despite having to battle doubts and racism. Many wonder how she did this, and to this, Wilma said, "I believe in me more than anything in this world."

Wilma proved that when you believe in yourself, you find an inner strength that will help you get far in whatever it is that you want to do. Believing in yourself is what gives you courage and what builds your confidence. Believing in yourself is the key to success.

Sadly, in 1994, Wilma passed away at the age of 54 due to a brain tumor. Wilma's life and work affected the whole world, despite her dying so young. Her impact can still be felt today in each little girl who chooses to pursue their dreams. It is incredible to think that this legend started as a young girl who once believed that she would never walk again.

During her career, she was known to say, "The triumph cannot be had without the struggle. And I know what struggle is. I have spent a lifetime trying to share what it has meant to be a woman first in the world of sports so that other young women have a chance to reach their dreams." And thanks to Wilma, every young woman — of any color, age, or ability — can do just that.

Hilary Knight

I believe Beyoncé said it best: Girls run the world! Many people might disagree with this idea, but ice hockey superstar Hilary Knight proves just how powerful a young girl with a dream can be and how much they can change the world when they set their mind to it.

Hilary was born on July 12, 1989, in Palo Alto, California. Even though she was a California native, her family moved to Lake Forest, Illinois, when she was young. Her family loved colder sports, especially skiing. But Hilary and her younger brothers decided to give something else a try instead — ice hockey.

It was a popular sport in the new area, but Hilary's parents had never ice skated before! They weren't sure how it would turn out, but they enrolled the children in the local community ice hockey league, and Hilary was immediately hooked.

When she was just five years old, Hilary told her grandmother that she was going to play hockey in the Olympics one day. Her grandmother told her, "Girls don't play hockey!" But Hilary, thankfully, didn't listen. She decided that girls could play hockey, and nothing would stop her from doing that. She understood something very important: girls can do whatever they want to do. Period.

Hilary's love for hockey was so great she would sleep with the three-inch pucks beneath her pillow for good luck. Can you imagine sleeping with a large, black disc under your head instead of a teddy bear? It must have been uncomfortable! But Hilary did it because she loved hockey and felt it would bring her good luck in the ice rink. Hilary was set up to be a champion from the start for sure!

Hilary put a lot of pressure on herself to be the best she could be from the very beginning. As the oldest child, she felt responsible for being a good example for her younger brothers. She wanted to be someone they could look up to both on and off the ice.

But while she showed a lot of skills in the hockey rink when she played, it wasn't easy being a girl playing a boys' sport. There were no girls' teams around her, so Hilary had to play on all-boys teams when she was young. Because she was the only girl, Hilary was bullied a lot by the boys on the team. She even had parents yelling at her from the stands because they didn't want a girl playing on their son's team! It was hard for a young girl to hear so many mean things just because she wanted to play hockey.

But these bullies only made Hilary more determined. Once she started beating boy after boy on her team, it was clear that Hilary was there to stay — and she was going to succeed in the sport no matter what those haters thought!

Hilary thanks her mother for this because she was a strong female role model for Hilary. Her mom motivated her to follow her passion to play ice hockey even though it was not considered a "woman's sport."

By the time she reached high school, Hilary had made a name for herself as a hockey player. After attending Choate Rosemary Hall and playing hockey all through high school, Hilary had her pick of any college she wanted. She was so good that many colleges wanted her on their teams! She chose the University of Wisconsin in Madison, and that is where she began her professional career.

Each season, she showed what a valuable player she was. She kept impressed everyone with her scoring skills as a forward. Ice hockey is a fast and rough game, so the fact that Hilary was so fantastic at scoring goals said a lot about her incredible skills on the ice.

She helped her team win two National Collegiate Athletic Association (NCAA) Championships and many other record achievements throughout college. When she graduated, she was immediately picked up to play for the Boston Blades in the Canadian Women's Hockey League (CWHL).

Hilary had an outstanding first season with the Blades and became the first American-born player to be named the Most Valuable Player. Over the next few years, Hilary bounced from team to team, showing the world how talented she truly was. She even became the first woman to be trained by an all-male team in the National Hockey League (NHL) with the Anaheim Ducks.

But Hilary's career has not just been about local championships. In 2010, she took a year off from her university commitments to train for the 2010 Olympic Games in Vancouver. She helped Team USA win a silver medal, and she now has a total of four Olympic medals—including one gold!

Hilary competed many times at the International Ice Hockey Federation (IIHF) World Women's Championship. She was even named the Most Valuable Player of the whole tournament in 2015! She has had more international success than any other woman, and is the only female hockey player to score over 100 points in her career. Hilary definitely made her mark on the sport very early on!

She was chosen to be the 2023 Women's World Championship team captain. This was her thirteenth World Championship, but it was her first game playing as the captain of her team. And Hilary led her team to a 7–1 victory.

It is always a great honor to be chosen to be a team captain. It shows just how much confidence your fellow players and coach have in your skills as a player and as a leader. She continued to do her best for the team and worked just as hard during the game as any of the other players.

While captain, she always tried her best to set a good example. To Hilary, everyone on the team has a special role to play, which makes each of them equally important. Hilary showed a lot of sportsmanship, because respecting her teammates gave added strength to them all. Hilary is a true team player!

During her early years as a professional women's hockey player, Hilary realized how important sponsorships are. Not only do sponsorships help athletes earn attention for their teams, but they are also a major part of their income. This was especially true for Hilary. Women's hockey leagues did not pay very well when Hilary first started. Her team actually paid so little that if Hilary had not earned some sponsorships, she might not have been able to afford to play hockey at all!

Ice hockey was still struggling to get recognition as a sport for women, which meant it didn't have a lot of money to give to its players the same way the National Hockey League did. Men's teams were far more supported and watched, so there was more money to give to male players.

Like Hilary's grandmother, many people in the world believed that women weren't meant to play hockey. So, there was a large difference between what women and men athletes in ice hockey were paid. Hilary knew how important sponsorships were to draw attention to this fact. Hilary said, "It was a lot of trial and error, but the biggest obstacle for me… was to tackle building a platform and getting seen."

Once she realized just how large the pay gap was between the National Women's Hockey League (NWHL) and the National Hockey League (NHL), Hilary became determined to change the way ice hockey worked. She recognized how unfair the pay differences were. Why should she be paid less just because she was a woman? The answer: she shouldn't!

Hilary became very outspoken about this matter. Then in 2017, Hilary and her teammates decided to make a real change. They threatened not to attend the World Championship if the pay gap between male and female teams was not fixed. What a bold move!

Both male and female leagues were set to lose a significant amount of money if this were to happen, and the players knew it. But it was worth the risk! To draw even more attention and support to this issue, Hilary started the #BeBoldForChange movement. She was determined to raise awareness for pay equality among male and female players.

After a long battle, Hilary and her team were successful! They were given equal pay to men and many other benefits, marking the beginning of a movement that improved equality between the male and female teams.

In 2019, many female players in the NWHL decided to form their own league to push for even better pay and standards for women's ice hockey. Then, the Professional Women's Players Hockey Association (PWPHA) was born.

As a player-led organization, the PWPHA makes sure all its players have the resources to train and have opportunities to compete on the same levels as other players. This worked alongside Hilary's aim to create a better future for young female players. She realized that all women deserve to have the same opportunities as men, which meant making sure they could make enough money to live well if they chose to play hockey professionally.

Because of her experiences as a young female player, Hilary decided that once she'd gained enough success, she could be a voice for change. As a young girl, she had been surrounded by powerful female role models who had inspired her to follow her dream and made her feel strong.

Hilary believes it is very important to surround yourself with positive role models. And she wanted nothing more than to become just that for other young girls by showing them how they can change the world despite what others might think.

In this world, many people have strict opinions about what women should be. Many believe that women are meant to only be mothers or wives and do nothing more than that — they certainly shouldn't become strong athletes.

While being mothers and wives are still great things to do, Hilary decided that this was not what she wanted for herself. She wanted to do what she loved. Now, Hilary doesn't just play hockey. In her spare time, she does all kinds of physical activities. She goes mountain biking, whitewater rafting, mountain climbing, and paddle boarding.

All of Hilary's activities are physical and active, which brought about a new kind of challenge: her strong, muscular body.

Because she is an athlete, Hilary has a challenging workout program. She has to focus a lot of her time on maintaining her body's core and leg strength so she can play her best. She also has to keep her body healthy by eating enough food throughout the day to keep her muscles strong.

This means that Hilary looks a little different than many other women. She has a muscular, strong body that only comes from working hard. Unfortunately, many have criticized her for her size, weight, and build because they believe women should look a certain way — thin and slim.

But Hilary said no to those opinions! No one could stop her from feeling proud to be a strong female athlete. The times of shaming people for having differently shaped bodies are over! All of our bodies are beautiful.

Hilary is not shy about showing off or being proud of her muscular body because she works hard for it. And she is just as beautiful as any other woman. She wanted to show that women should be comfortable with their body shape, whatever that shape might be.

She said, "It's okay to be fit and healthy and comfortable within your body, whatever frame you have. I've tried to shatter the body image that muscular isn't feminine."

Being feminine does not mean you have to be thin or weak. Women can have any body shape and size they want, and do any job they want, because they are strong and capable. A woman can be muscular and still be feminine. Being a strong woman is something to be proud of. And Hilary proves just that.

Hilary has made her mark on the ice rink and in every young girl's world. She has dedicated her life to making sure all female players get the equal treatment they deserve. She wants to be seen as a true spokesperson for change so that when little girls look up to her, they know they can achieve all their dreams.

And while many people challenge her, Hilary says, "I am a blue-sky thinker and dream big." She will not let others take down her dreams and control what she is capable of just because they have doubts. Thanks to women like Hilary, any girl with a "blue-sky" mindset can become whatever they want to be.

Conclusion

Weren't those stories inspiring? I feel like I can do just about anything!

Throughout history, and even now, women and girls have constantly been doubted in their ability to succeed and do what they set their minds to. But as we've just seen, that is simply not the case! Over and over again, women rise above challenges and conquer their dreams and goals!

Each of these women teaches us that being ourselves and following our dreams is the best thing we can do to make the world a better place.

Serena, Simone, Chloe, Ibtihaj, Maya, Jackie, and Wilma all showed the world that a person's value lies in their work, not their race. Tatyana and Bethany stood up against the odds and overcame disabilities so that they could pave their own ways in their sports. Megan, Hilary, and Leah proved just how powerful a woman can be when she uses her voice for something they believe in. And they all showed that women truly can do whatever they want to do and that challenges can turn a girl with a dream into a powerful woman.

There are always going to be challenges in life that will make us feel like we are not capable, like we are not strong enough. Each of these women shows us that is not true. Each woman's story proves how challenges turn us into stronger versions of ourselves, even if the world thinks we won't win.

No matter what, always remember that as a woman, you can:

Challenge the world like Serena.

Lead like a lioness like Leah.

Get back up like Simone.

Take pride in who you are like Chloe.

Break boundaries like Ibtihaj.

Fight for what you believe in like Maya.

Set world records like Jackie.

Be true to yourself like Megan.

Beat the odds like Tatyana.

Surprise the world like Bethany.

Overcome challenges like Wilma.

Have a "blue-sky" mind like Hilary.

Each of these women shows us how anyone can do what they set their minds to. Each woman had challenges, and each woman proved that we can all get back up, achieve our dreams, and make a difference in the world.

Above all, there is one quality that stands out among all these women: courage. With enough courage, you can be whoever and whatever you want to be. Women are strong. Women are capable. Women are inspirational. And you, too, can do whatever you set your mind to.

What great things would you like to achieve? In what ways will you change the world? Even in everyday life, like sitting at your desk at school or playing with your friends on the playground, can you change the world, one dream at a time?

I can't wait to see what you do!

Dear Wonderful Parents

I hope this message finds you well and that your child enjoyed reading my book! Writing this book was a labor of love, and I poured my heart into every chapter. As an independent author, your feedback means the world to me.

I would be immensely grateful if you could please take a few moments to share your thoughts in a review. Reviews are crucial in supporting authors like myself and helping other parents discover this book. I genuinely read every review and am excited to hear your thoughts.

Thank you!

Jessica Blakely

Ready to share your thoughts? Scan one of the QR codes below:

Amazon US

Amazon UK

Amazon Canada

Amazon Australia

References

A&E Television Networks. (2021, April 23). *Serena Williams*. Biography. https://www.biography.com/athletes/serena-williams

A&E Television Networks. (2021, April 23). *Wilma Rudolph*. Biography. https://www.biography.com/athletes/wilma-rudolph

A&E Television Networks. (2021, May 5). *Jackie Joyner-Kersee*. Biography. https://www.biography.com/athletes/jackie-joyner-kersee

A&E Television Networks. (2022, September 12). *Ibtihaj Muhammad*. Biography. https://www.biography.com/athlete/ibtihaj-muhammad

About Maya. Maya Moore. Retrieved January 15, 2024, from https://mayamoore.com/about/

Amrani, I. (2023, September 18). *US Olympian Ibtihaj Muhammad: I showed what Muslim women can do in sport*. Al Jazeera. https://www.aljazeera.com/sports/2023/9/18/ibtihaj-muhammad-fencing-olympics-muslim-women-sport#

Barnes, K. (2023, January 16). *Maya Moore Legacy Extends Far Beyond Basketball Court*. ESPN. https://www.espn.com/wnba/story/_/id/35460003/maya-moore-wnba-retirement-legacy-basketball-justice

Barton, S. (2023, June 17). *Leah Williamson Biography*. Footbalium. https://footbalium.com/lifestyle/biography/17513-leah-williamson-biography/

Bethany Hamilton. Retrieved January 15, 2024, from https://bethanyh amilton.com/

BrainyQuote. *Chloe Kim Quotes*. Brainy Quotes. Retrieved January 15, 2024, from https://www.brainyquote.com/authors/chloe-kim-quotes

Brandman, M. *Ibtihaj Muhammad*. National Women's History Museum. Retrieved January 15, 2024, from https://www.womenshistory.org/education-resources/biographies/ibtihaj-muhammad

Brandman, M. *Serena Williams*. National Women's History Museum. Retrieved January 15, 2024, from https://www.womenshistory.org/education-resources/biographies/serena-williams

Britannica, T. Editors of Encyclopaedia (2023, December 10). *Chloe Kim*. Encyclopedia Britannica. https://www.britannica.com/biography/Chloe-Kim

Britannica, T. Editors of Encyclopaedia (2023, December 15). *Wilma Rudolph*. Encyclopedia Britannica. https://www.britannica.com/biography/Wilma-Rudolph

Britannica, T. Editors of Encyclopaedia (2023, December 26). *Serena Williams*. Encyclopedia Britannica. https://www.britannica.com/biography/Serena-Williams

Britannica, T. Editors of Encyclopaedia (2023, December 7). *Jackie Joyner-Kersee*. Encyclopedia Britannica. https://www.britannica.com/biography/Jackie-Joyner-Kersee

Britannica, T. Editors of Encyclopaedia (2023, November 30). *Megan Rapinoe*. Encyclopædia Britannica. https://www.britannica.com/biography/Megan-Rapinoe

REFERENCES

Brown, S. M. (2020, March 4). *Serena Williams Builds Schools in Jamaica, Africa*. Heart & Soul. https://www.heartandsoul.com/celebrity/serena-williams-builds-schools-in-jamaica-africa/

Caron, E. (2022, February 16). *Olympic Star Hilary Knight Builds Brand, Looks Beyond the Rink*. Sportico. https://www.sportico.com/leagues/hockey/2022/hilary-knight-brand-beijing-olympics-1234661866/

Carroll, E. *Jackie Joyner-Kersee: Biography & Quotes*. Study.com. Retrieved January 15, 2024, from https://study.com/academy/lesson/jackie-joyner-kersee-biography-quotes.html

Chloe Kim. U.S. Ski & Snowboard. Retrieved January 15, 2024, from https://usskiandsnowboard.org/athletes/chloe-kim

Commins, L. (2018, January 11). *14 Things to Know About Hilary Knight, Team USA's Hockey Player and Equal Pay Activist*. Cosmopolitan. https://www.cosmopolitan.com/entertainment/celebs/a13796167/hilary-knight-hockey-olympics/

Crawford, A. (2016, September 21). *Bravo, Simone Biles, for Taking a Stand Against ADHD Stigma*. ESPN. https://www.espn.com/espnw/voices/story/_/id/17602540/bravo-simone-biles-taking-stand-adhd-stigma

Donahue, A. B. (2022, April 11). *What You Need to Know About Wheelchair Racing*. Invacare. https://www.passionatepeople.invacare.eu.com/need-know-wheelchair-racing/

Dye, N. (2023, October 9). *Simone Biles "Didn't Think" She'd Ever Compete Again Before Becoming Most Decorated Gymnast of All-Time*. People. https://people.com/simone-biles-reveals-that-she-didnt-think-shed-ever-compete-again-8349303

Emery, L. (2017, January 24). *The Unbeatable Advocate: Tatyana McFadden*. Runner's World. https://www.runnersworld.com/runners-stories/a20843533/the-unbeatable-advocate-tatyana-mcfadden/

Fandom, Inc. *Chloe Kim*. Muppet Wiki. Retrieved January 15, 2024, from 15https://muppet.fandom.com/wiki/Chloe_Kim

Gilby, B. (2023, February 15). *Leah Williamson: Promoting equality and togetherness*. Impetus Football. https://impetusfootball.org/2023/02/15/leah-williamson-promoting-equality-and-togetherness/

Guardian News & Media. (2013, July 27). *Tatyana McFadden wins six from six in Paralympic clean sweep in Lyon*. The Guardian. https://www.theguardian.com/sport/2013/jul/27/tatyana-mcfadden-paralympic-six-gold-medals

Harkin, S. (2020, November 11). *Serena Williams Biography for Kids*. Lottie Dolls US. https://www.lottie.com/blogs/strong-women/serena-williams

Harkin, S. (2021, July 20). *Maya Moore Biography for Kids*. Lottie Dolls US. https://www.lottie.com/blogs/strong-women/maya-moore-biography-for-kids

Harkin, S. (2021, May 5). *Simone Biles Biography for kids*. Lottie Dolls US. https://www.lottie.com/blogs/strong-women/simone-biles-biography-for-kids

Herrera, S. (2023, October 6). *Megan Rapinoe's top 10 iconic moments: The unforgettable goals, quotes, hair colors, celebrations and more*. CBS Sports. https://www.cbssports.com/soccer/news/megan-rapinoes-top-10-moments-ahead-of-her-last-uswnt-match-the-highlights-that-defined-a-storied-career/

Hilary Knight. Retrieved January 15, 2024, from https://www.hilaryknight.com/#home-section

Hirsch, A. (2022, September 3). *Serena Williams showed the world that Black Women Excel. That has changed us all*. The

Guardian. https://www.theguardian.com/commentisfree/2022/sep/03/serena-williams-black-women-tennis-champion

Ibtihaj Muhammad. Retrieved January 15, 2024, from https://www.ibtihajmuhammad.com/

Irons, M. M., & Irons, J. (2023). *Love and Justice: A Story of Triumph on Two Different Courts*. Disney Publishing Worldwide.

Jobs In Football. (2022, September 15). *20 Megan Rapinoe Quotes to Inspire & Motivate*. https://jobsinfootball.com/blog/megan-rapinoe-quotes/

Lake, T., & Hibler, J. (2023, December 8). *Bethany Hamilton*. Encyclopædia Britannica. https://www.britannica.com/biography/Bethany-Hamilton

Lavietes, M. (2022, July 7). *Soccer Star Megan Rapinoe Receives Presidential Medal of Freedom*. NBC News. https://www.nbcnews.com/nbc-out/nbc-out-proud/soccer-star-megan-rapinoe-receives-presidential-medal-freedom-rcna37141

Leah Williamson. Arsenal. Retrieved January 15, 2024, from https://www.arsenal.com/women/players/leah-williamson

Lev. (2023, July 11). *Heptathlon Sport Rules*. Game Rules. https://gamerules.com/rules/heptathlon-sport-rules/

Lewis, J. J. (2020, January 14). *Biography of Jackie Joyner-Kersee, Record-Setting Olympic Athlete*. LiveAbout. https://www.liveabout.com/jackie-joyner-kersee-3529410

Linehan, M. (2022, May 26). *Hilary Knight takes control: Her identity, her dreams and the fight for what's next*. The Athletic. https://theathletic.com/3334156/2022/05/26/hilary-knight/

LoRé, M. (2021, August 19). *Tatyana McFadden Talks 2020 Paralympics, Mental Health and Overcoming a Career-Threatening Condition*. Forbes. https://www.forbes.com/sites/michaellore/2021/08/19/tatyana-mcfadden-talks-2020-paralympics-mental-health-and-overcoming-a-career-threatening-condition/?sh=59392b29b501

Manasan, A. (2021, April 11). *Coming out "made me a better, more full person," says U.S. Soccer Star Megan Rapinoe*. CBC. https://www.cbc.ca/radio/sunday/the-sunday-magazine-for-november-29-2020-1.5817667/coming-out-made-me-a-better-more-full-person-says-u-s-soccer-star-megan-rapinoe-1.5819650

Martin, B. (2023, January 16). *The Magic of Maya Moore: The Career of a True Champion*. WNBA. https://www.wnba.com/news/the-magic-of-maya-moore-the-career-of-a-true-champion

McCarvel, N. (2015, December 15). *Serena Williams revels in Sports illustrated cover limelight*. USA Today. https://www.usatoday.com/story/sports/tennis/2015/12/15/serena-williams-explains-idea-behind-sports-illustrated-cover/77391104/

McFadden, T., & Walker, T. (2016). *Ya Sama! Moments from My Life*. Inspired Edge Publications.

McLeod, N. S. (2020, May 18). *60 Simone Biles Quotes for the Powerful Olympian in You*. Everyday Power. https://everydaypower.com/simone-biles-quotes/

Mead, W. (2023, October 5). *Simone Biles*. Biography. https://www.biography.com/athletes/simone-biles

Meriweather, M. W. (2022, August 29). *A Look Back at Serena Williams's Best*. InStyle. https://www.instyle.com/celebrity/serena-williams/serena-williams-tennis-fashion-legacy

REFERENCES

Merrell, C. (2021, December 9). *The Most Asked Questions about Chloe Kim*. Olympics.com. https://olympics.com/en/news/the-most-asked-questions-about-chloe-kim

Muhammad, I. (2020). *The Proudest Blue: A story of hijab and family*. Findaway World, LLC.

National Women's Hall of Fame. *Wilma Rudolph*. National Women's Hall of Fame. Retrieved January 15, 2024, from https://www.womenofthehall.org/inductee/wilma-rudolph/

NBC Sports. (2022, July 7). *Simone Biles, Megan Rapinoe join Olympians to receive Presidential Medal of Freedom*. NBC Sports. https://www.nbcsports.com/olympics/news/simone-biles-megan-rapinoe-presidential-medal-of-freedom

New York Road Runners, Inc. *Tatyana McFadden*. New York Road Runners. Retrieved January 15, 2024, from https://www.nyrr.org/media-center/athletes/tatyana-mcfadden

Norwood, A. R. (2017). *Wilma Rudolph*. National Women's History Museum. https://www.womenshistory.org/education-resources/biographies/wilma-rudolph

O'Brien, P. (2023, August 9). *Hilary Knight Powers Women's hockey on and off the ice*. Adirondack Daily Enterprise. https://www.adirondackdailyenterprise.com/sports/local-sports/2023/08/hilary-knight-powers-womens-hockey-on-and-off-the-ice/

Olympics.com. *Chloe Kim*. Olympics.com. Retrieved January 15, 2024, from https://olympics.com/en/athletes/chloe-kim

Olympics.com. *Jackie Joyner-Kersee*. Olympics.com. Retrieved January 15, 2024, from https://olympics.com/en/athletes/jackie-joyner-kersee

Olympics.com. *Serena Williams*. Olympics.com. Retrieved January 15, 2024, from https://olympics.com/en/athletes/serena-williams

Ott, T. (2021, September 29). *Bethany Hamilton*. Biography. https://www.biography.com/athletes/bethany-hamilton

Our Athletes Are for Active Schools. Athletes for Hope. (2016, October 13). https://www.athletesforhope.org/2016/10/athletes-active-schools/

Peszek, L. (2023, December 22). *Simone Biles*. Encyclopedia Britannica. https://www.britannica.com/biography/Simone-Biles

Picotti, T. (2023, September 25). *Megan Rapinoe*. Biography. https://www.biography.com/athletes/megan-rapinoe

Radnofsky, L. (2023, October 9). *Simone Biles Is Officially the Most Decorated Gymnast in History*. Mint. https://www.livemint.com/sports/simone-biles-is-officially-the-most-decorated-gymnast-in-history-11696851782431.html

Rioux, M. (2023, April 22). *Leah Williamson Biography – Childhood, Parents, Family [2024]*. Soccer Bio. https://soccerbiography.com/leah-williamson/

Roberts, M. B. *Rudolph Ran and World Went Wild*. ESPN. Retrieved January 15, 2024, from https://www.espn.com/classic/biography/s/Rudolph_Wilma.html

Roenigk, A. (2022, April 2). *Olympic Gold Medalist Chloe Kim Shares Her Experiences with Anti-Asian Hate*. ESPN. https://www.espn.com/olympics/story/_/id/31182888/olympic-gold-medalist-chloe-kim-shares-experience-anti-asian-hate

Rowbottom, M. (2020, August 2). *Rising Phoenix - telling the whole story of Paralympic champions such as McFadden, Vio and Peacock*. Inside the

Games. https://www.insidethegames.biz/articles/1096932/rising-phoenix-netflix-paralympics-film

Schlinger, A. (2013, August 22). *Bethany Hamilton: Soul Surfer and Fitness Inspiration*. Daily Burn. https://dailyburn.com/life/fitness/bethany-hamilton-soul-surfer/

Scipioni, J. (2021, August 26). *Growing up disabled in a Russian orphanage: How Tatyana McFadden became one of the fastest women in the world*. CNBC Make It. https://www.cnbc.com/2021/08/26/tatyana-mcfadden-from-orphan-to-fastest-woman-in-the-world.html

Serena Williams Story for Kids. Bedtime History: Podcast and Videos for Kids. (2023, April 9). https://bedtimehistorystories.com/serena-williams-story-for-kids/

Simone Biles Facts, Worksheets, Olympics, Life & Biography for Kids. KidsKonnect. (2021, August 9). https://kidskonnect.com/people/simone-biles/

Simone Biles. Academy of Achievement. (2023, October 6). https://achievement.org/achiever/simone-biles/

Simone Biles. Retrieved January 15, 2024, from https://simonebiles.com/about/

Sky UK. (2024, January 12). *Leah Williamson: Arsenal defender back in full training as she continues recovery from ACL Injury*. Sky Sports. https://www.skysports.com/football/news/11670/13046886/leah-williamson-arsenal-defender-back-in-full-training-as-she-continues-recovery-from-acl-injury

Soccer Training Info. (2019, June 26). *How to Play Like Megan Rapinoe*. https://soccer-training-info.com/how_to_play_like_megan_rapinoe/

SurferToday.com. *37 Interesting Facts about Bethany Hamilton*. Surfer Today. Retrieved January 15, 2024, from https://www.surfertoday.com/surfing/interesting-facts-about-bethany-hamilton

Swensen, E. (2003, September 18). *Olympian Promotes Asthma Care\ Jackie Joyner-Kersee Overcame the Breathing Disease To Win Six Olympic Medals.* Greensboro News and Record. https://greensboro.com/olympian-promotes-asthma-care-jackie-joyner-kersee-overcame-the-breathing-disease-to-win-six-olympic/article_8c57f24e-10d9-5095-8677-8b4cc0bfb09f.html

Tatyana McFadden. Retrieved January 15, 2024, https://tatyanamcfadden.com/about-tatyana

Team USA Hockey. *Hilary Knight*. Team USA: USA Hockey. Retrieved January 15, 2024, from https://teamusa.usahockey.com/2022olympics-hilaryknight

Tempera, J. (2022, February 8). *Chloe Kim's Dad Has Supported Her Olympic Dreams Since She Was A Child—He Even Quit His Job For Her*. Women's Health. https://www.womenshealthmag.com/life/a39015030/chloe-kim-parents-dad-commercial/

The Football Association. *Leah Williamson*. England Football. Retrieved January 15, 2024, from https://www.englandfootball.com/england/womens-senior-team/squad/leah-williamson

The Football Association. *Leah Williamson: My first club*. Women's Leagues and Competitions. Retrieved January 15, 2024, from https://womenscompetitions.thefa.com/en/Article/leah-williamson-arsenal-england-scot-youth-121018

The Peter Westbrook Foundation. Retrieved January 15, 2024, from https://www.peterwestbrook.org/

REFERENCES

The Washington Post. (1993, June 10). *Joyner-Kersee Breathes a Bit Easier After Scare*. The Washington Post. https://www.washingtonpost.com/archive/sports/1993/06/10/joyner-kersee-breathes-a-bit-easier-after-scare/8a88d912-6a69-47c4-96e0-3dc999d761c3/

Tiefenthaler, C. (2021, February 23). *Ibtihaj Muhammad: More than a medalist*. IGNITE. https://ignitenational.org/blog/ibtihaj-muhammad-more-than-a-medalist

Top 20 Serena Williams Quotes to Inspire You to Rise Up and Win. Goalcast. (2022, September 2). https://www.goalcast.com/top-20-serena-williams-quotes-to-inspire-you-to-rise-up-win/

U.S. Soccer. (2023, July 8). *U.S. Women's National Team Legend Megan Rapinoe Announces Retirement from Professional Soccer at End of 2023 NWSL Season*. U.S. Soccer Official Website. https://www.ussoccer.com/stories/2023/07/us-womens-national-team-legend-megan-rapinoe-will-retire-at-end-of-2023-nwsl-season

United States Olympic & Paralympic Committee. *Tatyana McFadden*. Team USA. Retrieved January 15, 2024, from https://www.teamusa.com/profiles/tatyana-mcfadden-800356

Western, D. (2016, November 30). *5 Strong Success Lessons from Serena Williams*. SUCCESS. https://www.success.com/5-strong-success-lessons-from-serena-williams/

Who is Serena Williams? Twinkl. Retrieved January 15, 2024, from https://www.twinkl.com/teaching-wiki/serena-williams#:~:text=Serena%20Williams%20is%20an%20American,woman%20during%20the%20open%20era.

Wikimedia Foundation, Inc. (2023, December 23). *Maya Moore*. Wikipedia, the Free Encyclopedia. https://en.wikipedia.org/wiki/Maya_Moore

Wikimedia Foundation, Inc. (2024, January 12). *Hilary Knight.* Wikipedia, the Free Encyclopedia. https://en.wikipedia.org/wiki/Hilary_Knight_(ice_hockey)

Wikimedia Foundation, Inc. (2024, January 12). *Ibtihaj Muhammad.* Wikipedia, the Free Encyclopedia. https://en.wikipedia.org/wiki/Ibtihaj_Muhammad

Wikimedia Foundation, Inc. (2024, January 13). *Megan Rapinoe.* Wikipedia, the Free Encyclopedia. https://en.wikipedia.org/wiki/Megan_Rapinoe

Wikimedia Foundation, Inc. (2024, January 4). *Bethany Hamilton.* Wikipedia, the Free Encyclopedia. https://en.wikipedia.org/wiki/Bethany_Hamilton

Wikimedia Foundation, Inc. (2024, January 8). *Wilma Rudolph.* Wikipedia, the Free Encyclopedia. https://en.wikipedia.org/wiki/Wilma_Rudolph

Wikimedia Foundation, Inc. (2024, January 9). *Leah Williamson.* Wikipedia, the Free Encyclopedia. https://en.wikipedia.org/wiki/Leah_Williamson

Wikimedia Foundation, Inc. (n.d.). *Maya Moore.* Basketball Wiki. Retrieved January 15, 2024, from https://basketball.fandom.com/wiki/Maya_Moore

Williamson, L., & Wrack, S. (2023). *You Have the Power.* Macmillan Children's Books.

Wilma Rudolph: Olympic Legend. Wilma Rudolph. (2022, May 16). http://wilmarudolph.com/

Wilson, J. (2020, June 11). *US Soccer repeals 2017 rule that banned kneeling during the national anthem.* The Guardian. https://www.theguardian.com/football/2020/jun/10/us-soccer-repeals-anthem-kneeling-rule

Printed in Great Britain
by Amazon